INTRODUCING
ISSUES WITH
OPPOSING
VIEWPOINTS®

D0003624

Bullying

Other books in the Introducing Issues
with Opposing Viewpoints series:

AIDS
Civil Liberties
Cloning
The Death Penalty
Gangs
Gay Marriage
Genetic Engineering
Smoking
Terrorism

**INTRODUCING
ISSUES WITH
OPPOSING
VIEWPOINTS**®

Bullying

Beth Rosenthal, *Book Editor*

Christine Nasso, *Publisher*
Elizabeth Des Chenes, *Managing Editor*

GREENHAVEN PRESS
A part of Gale, Cengage Learning

GALE
CENGAGE Learning™

Detroit • New York • San Francisco • New Haven, Conn • Waterville, Maine • London

© 2008, Greenhaven Press, a part of Gale, Cengage Learning.

For more information, contact
Greenhaven Press
27500 Drake Rd.
Farmington Hills, MI 48331-3535
Or you can visit our Internet site at http://www.gale.com

LIBRARY OF CONGRESS CATALOGING-IN-PUBLICATION DATA

Bullying / Beth Rosenthal, book editor.
   p. cm. — (Introducing issues with opposing viewpoints)
  Includes bibliographical references and index.
  ISBN-13: 978-0-7377-3801-8 (hardcover)
 1. Bullying. I. Rosenthal, Beth, 1964-
  BF637.B85B84 2008
  302.3—dc22

                       2007032382

ISBN-10: 0-7377-3801-4 (hardcover)

Printed in the United States of America
 2 3 4 5 6 7 12 11 10 09 08

Contents

Chapter 3: How Can Bullying Be Reduced?

Foreword

Indulging in a wide spectrum of ideas, beliefs, and perspectives is a critical cornerstone of democracy. After all, it is often debates over differences of opinion, such as whether to legalize abortion, how to treat prisoners, or when to enact the death penalty that shape our society and drive it forward. Such diversity of thought is frequently regarded as the hallmark of a healthy and civilized culture. As the Reverend Clifford Schutjer of the First Congregational Church in Mansfield, Ohio, declared in a 2001 sermon, "Surrounding oneself with only like-minded people, restricting what we listen to or read only to what we find agreeable is irresponsible. Refusing to entertain doubts once we make up our minds is a subtle but deadly form of arrogance." With this advice in mind, Introducing Issues with Opposing Viewpoints books aim to open readers' minds to the critically divergent views that comprise our world's most important debates.

Introducing Issues with Opposing Viewpoints simplifies for students the enormous and often overwhelming mass of material now available via print and electronic media. Collected in every volume is an array of opinions that capture the essence of a particular controversy or topic. Introducing Issues with Opposing Viewpoints books embody the spirit of nineteenth-century journalist Charles A. Dana's axiom: "Fight for your opinions, but do not believe that they contain the whole truth, or the only truth." Absorbing such contrasting opinions teaches students to analyze the strength of an argument and compare it to its opposition. From this process readers can inform and strengthen their own opinions, or be exposed to new information that will change their minds. Introducing Issues with Opposing Viewpoints is a mosaic of different voices. The authors are statesmen, pundits, academics, journalists, corporations, and ordinary people who have felt compelled to share their experiences and ideas in a public forum. Their words have been collected from newspapers, journals, books, speeches, interviews, and the Internet, the fastest growing body of opinionated material in the world.

Introducing Issues with Opposing Viewpoints shares many of the well-known features of its critically acclaimed parent series, Opposing Viewpoints. The articles are presented in a pro/con format, allowing readers to absorb divergent perspectives side by side. Active reading questions preface each viewpoint, requiring the student to approach the material thoughtfully and carefully. Useful charts, graphs, and cartoons supplement each article. A thorough introduction provides readers with crucial background on an issue. An annotated bibliography points the reader toward articles, books, and Web sites that contain additional information on the topic. An appendix of organizations to contact contains a wide variety of charities, nonprofit organizations, political groups, and private enterprises that each hold a position on the issue at hand. Finally, a comprehensive index allows readers to locate content quickly and efficiently.

Introducing Issues with Opposing Viewpoints is also significantly different from Opposing Viewpoints. As the series title implies, its presentation will help introduce students to the concept of opposing viewpoints, and learn to use this material to aid in critical writing and debate. The series' four-color, accessible format makes the books attractive and inviting to readers of all levels. In addition, each viewpoint has been carefully edited to maximize a reader's understanding of the content. Short but thorough viewpoints capture the essence of an argument. A substantial, thought-provoking essay question placed at the end of each viewpoint asks the student to further investigate the issues raised in the viewpoint, compare and contrast two authors' arguments, or consider how one might go about forming an opinion on the topic at hand. Each viewpoint contains sidebars that include at-a-glance information and handy statistics. A Facts About section located in the back of the book further supplies students with relevant facts and figures.

Following in the tradition of the Opposing Viewpoints series, Greenhaven Press continues to provide readers with invaluable exposure to the controversial issues that shape our world. As John Stuart Mill once wrote: "The only way in which a human being can make some approach to knowing the whole of a subject is by hearing what can be said about it by persons of every variety of opinion and studying all modes in which it can be looked at by every character of mind. No wise man ever acquired his wisdom in any mode but this." It is to this principle that Introducing Issues with Opposing Viewpoints books are dedicated.

Introduction

Breaking the cycle of violence involves more than merely identifying and stopping the bully. It requires that we examine why and how a child becomes a bully or a target of a bully (and sometimes both) as well as the role bystanders play in perpetuating the cycle.

—Barbara Coloroso, *The Bully, the Bullied, and the Bystander*

Bullying continues to be a troubling—and growing—problem in our society. While everyone agrees that steps need to be taken to reduce bullying, there is no consensus on how to achieve this. Seung-Hui Cho's killing of thirty-two people at Virginia Polytechnic Institute and State University (Virginia Tech) on April 16, 2007, is only the latest example of someone who was bullied as a child turning to the ultimate revenge.

Why do children bully others? According to the U.S. Health Resources and Services Administration's Stop Bullying Now! Web site: Children bully "because I see others doing it, because it's what you do if you want to hang out with the right crowd, because it makes me feel stronger, smarter, or better than the person I'm bullying, and because it's one of the best ways to keep others from bullying me." This leaves the bullied child feeling, in many cases, not only hopeless and helpless, but also confused as to why he or she is being picked on.

As a child in Canada's Kids Help Phone's March 2006 Bullying Research Report said: "My entire class hates me. They all make fun of me and are really mean to me. They make fun of me for everything from talking to this kid who everyone hates cause he's really different to getting one question wrong or something. No matter what I do they make fun of me. Everything I say I get teased about so I stopped talking during school altogether and they make fun of me for that. . . . It's like I don't even exist. Like when I'm doing group work the other group members decide to change something and they don't tell me. But everyone else in the group knows. So it's like they completely forget about me. . . . Why does everyone hate me?"

Kids are bullied in school or online by other students, or at home by their siblings or parents. It doesn't always stop when kids grow up. A March 2007 poll by the Employment Law Alliance found that "the grade school bully may have grown up to become the office oppressor," in which almost 45 percent of American workers report that they have been bullied at work.

As access to the Internet has become increasingly common, so, too, has the opportunity for a new kind of torment—cyberbullying. Perhaps because it is an indirect form of harassment, it is possible that bullies do not realize that the grief inflicted on the bullied is just as painful as when the bullying is done face-to-face. An online survey of 1,500 teenagers conducted by Sameer Hinduja and Justin W. Patchin in 2005 found that 50 percent of respondents stated that "cyberbullying is done in fun," 22.2 percent believed that "cyberbullying teaches victims something," and 13 percent believed that "bullying makes victims stronger."

What can be done to help children who face constant bullying? As bullied children become more desperate about their situation, thoughts of violence and suicide can take over. The American Academy of Child and Adolescent Psychiatry reports on its Web site that "suicide is the third leading cause of death for 15-to-24-year-olds, and the sixth leading cause of death for 5-to-14-year-olds." Brenda High's son, Jared, committed suicide after enduring years of bullying in school. As she writes on her Web site, www.jaredstory.com: "The act of being bullied tends to increase some students' isolation because their peers do not want to lose status by associating with them or because they do not want to increase the risks of being bullied themselves."

The Olweus Bullying Prevention Program and Izzy Kalman's Bullies 2 Buddies program are two examples of the divide between widely divergent views about how to help the bullied and reduce bullying. Dr. Dan Olweus created the Olweus Bullying Prevention Program, which is used in schools around the world and involves the parents of the bullied, bullies, and bystanders, schools and classrooms, and communities to teach and reinforce positive behavior and how to react appropriately to bullying.

Izzy Kalman, a school psychologist, takes the view that bullied children must stand up for themselves by trying to befriend those doing the bullying. He believes that anti-bullying programs do not work and are counterproductive because, as he states on his Web site, www .bullies2buddies.com, "If victims have to rely on others to protect them from bullies, they may be bullied for the rest of their lives." Kalman doesn't feel that bullies recognize themselves to be bullies and, thus, will not change; therefore, it is up to the bully's victim to assert him- or herself to take control of the situation.

Introducing Issues with Opposing Viewpoints: Bullying explores the debate over bullying in our society. Topics covered include its causes, such as the role society plays in encouraging bullying, whether or not video games contribute to it, and whether bullying is learned from parents and television; the part parents and society can play in fighting it; whether homeschooling is an effective deterrent; parents' responsibility; using the Internet and legislation to fight it; ways in which bullying can be reduced; the pros and cons of anti-bullying laws; and using lunchtime recess to reduce the problem. Bullying is a highly complex issue; there are as many proposed solutions for preventing it as there are reasons for it taking place in the first place. As long as children (and adults, for that matter) have the need to feel superior to and more powerful than others, as long as the bullied continue to feel anger and despair, and as long as others simply stand by and watch the bullying without taking action, the cycle of violence will continue.

Chapter 1

What Causes Bullying?

The television show, "Everybody Hates Chris," is based on Chris Rock's teen years and depicts the kind of the bullying he experienced in junior high school.

Viewpoint

1

Bullies and Their Victims: A Violent Culture

Sue Smith-Heavenrich

Living in a culture that encourages competition and dominance, most Americans do not take bullying seriously.

In the following viewpoint, author Sue Smith-Heavenrich discusses how society has allowed bullying, which includes verbally and/or physically picking on others, to become acceptable. She argues that we live in a culture that does not take bullying seriously, and thus has resulted in a reported 90 percent of middle school and 66 percent of high school students that have been bullied during their school careers. She also claims that being a bully is hazardous to one's health and that the people most hurt by the bullying are ultimately the bullies themselves. Sue Smith-Heavenrich is a writer for *Mothering Magazine*, which published this article.

AS YOU READ, CONSIDER THE FOLLOWING QUESTIONS:

1. According to the article, approximately how many children miss school each day for fear of being bullied?
2. What are some physical and emotional ways in which a bully might pick on others?
3. What does Sue Smith-Heavenrich state are some of the ways in which the bullies themselves are hurt by bullying?

Sue Smith-Heavenrich, "Kids Hurting Kids: Bullies in the Schoolyard." *Mothering Magazine*, Issue 106, May/June 2001.

Bullying, often dismissed as a normal part of growing up, is a real problem in our nation's schools, according to the National School Safety Center. One out of every four schoolchildren endures taunting, teasing, pushing, and shoving daily from schoolyard bullies. More than 43 percent of middle- and high-school students avoid using school bathrooms for fear of being harassed or assaulted. Old-fashioned schoolyard hazing has escalated to instances of extortion, emotional terrorism, and kids toting guns to school.

Bullying exists in every Western or Westernized culture, from Finland and Australia to Japan and China. Three million bullying incidents are reported each year in the US alone, and over 160,000 children miss school each day for fear of being bullied. In Japan, bullying is called *ijime*. In 1993, just months before three suicides pushed ijime into the headlines, there were over 21,500 reported incidents of schoolyard bullying.

Culture Has Allowed Bullying to Become Acceptable

Many who flee urban streets to escape the culture of violence learn too late that bullying is more common in rural areas than in the cities. Researchers who surveyed hundreds of children living in the rural American Midwest found that 90 percent of middle school students and 66 percent of high school students reported having been bullied during their school careers.

The violent imagery in this drawing was produced by one of the teens responsible for the Columbine High School massacre.

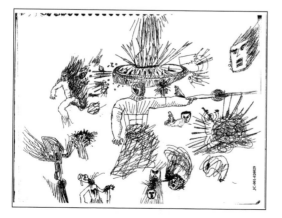

Living in a culture that encourages competition and dominance, most Americans do not take bullying seriously. The problem, says UCLA Adjunct Associate Professor of Psychology Jaana Juvonen, is that ridicule and intimidation have become acceptable. Her studies indicate that starting in middle school, bullies are considered "cool," while their victims are rejected from the social milieu.

It is estimated that more than 90 percent of all incidents of school violence begin with verbal conflicts, which escalate to profanities and then to fists or worse. Our culture has a great degree of tolerance for violence as a solution to problems. Just stroll through the local toy store; you'll find star destroyers, robots that shred their enemies, and even dolls dressed in black trench coats, wearing ski masks and toting guns. It should come as no surprise, then, that the US ranks along with England, Ireland, and Canada as having more bullies per capita than just about anywhere else in the world.

Meet the Bullies

A bully is someone who verbally or physically picks on others. A school bully might push you out of your seat, kick you when your back is turned, demand lunch money, threaten or insult you, call you names, or make jokes about you. A bully might give you dirty looks and spread rumors about you.

In addition to physical violence, threats, and name-calling are behaviors that qualify as emotional bullying. Excluding a child from

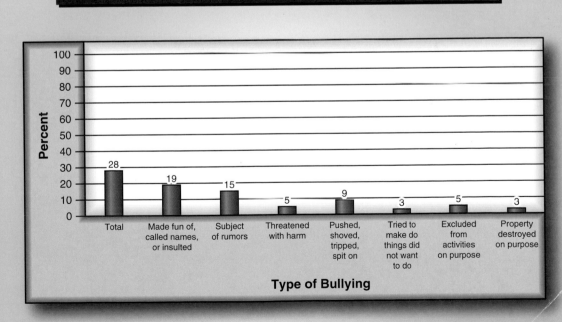

Children Ages 12–18 Who Were Bullied at School

Taken from: U.S. Department of Justice, Bureau of Justice Statistics, School Crime Supplement (SCS) to the National Crime Victimization Survey, 2005.

FAST FACT

According to the Southern California Center of Excellence on Youth Violence Prevention, kids who are recognized as bullies by age eight are six times more likely to commit a crime by the time they are twenty-four and five times more likely to have a serious criminal record by age thirty.

a group or tormenting, ridiculing, and humiliating someone are kinds of emotional violence. Bullying can be racist in nature, with slurs, taunts, graffiti, and gestures. It can be sexual, with one child making abusive comments or pushing unwanted physical contact on another.

Bullies try to shame and intimidate their victims and make them feel inadequate. Some bullies are active and aggressive; others are reserved and manipulative, relying on smooth talk and lies. Bullying is not gender specific; it is estimated that 25 percent of bullies are females. Regardless of how big they are or what they look like, all bullies want power and have difficulty seeing things from another person's perspective. Simply put, bullies use other people to get what they want. Researchers are now finding out that bullies are different from other children. Their aggression begins at an early age, and they tend to attribute hostile intentions to others. They perceive provocation where none exists and set out to exact revenge. Eventually they come to believe that aggression is their best solution to conflicts.

Formerly it was accepted that bullying was rooted in low self-esteem. Recent research by UCLA's Juvonen and others reveals, however, that bullies tend to regard themselves in a positive light. Up to about sixth grade they are fairly popular, but as they get older their popularity wanes. By the time they're in high school, they tend to hang out with others like themselves: self-styled tough guys who may get what they want but are not well liked.

Bullies Suffer in The Long Run

The person most hurt by bullying is often not the victim but the bully. The bully's behavior interferes with learning and friendships, and later on with work, relationships, income, and mental health. Children who bully tend to turn into antisocial adults and are more likely to commit crimes, batter spouses, and abuse their children. One study shows that 60 percent of boys who were bullies in middle school had at least one court conviction by the age of 24.

One researcher followed the lives of 518 individuals from the age of eight to about 50. Those children who were labeled as bullies went on to receive more driving citations and court convictions and showed higher rates of alcoholism and antisocial personality disorders. Though their intelligence level in the early grades was on a par with that of other children, by the time they were 19, their aggressive behavior interfered with developing intellectual skills. In high school, these were the children who experimented more with sex, drugs, and alcohol and had higher dropout rates.

About one third of bullies are themselves victims of bullying, and a recent study shows that these children have a higher risk of depression and suicidal thoughts than other children. Clearly, being a bully can be hazardous to your health.

EVALUATING THE AUTHOR'S ARGUMENTS:

In the viewpoint you just read, author Sue Smith-Heavenrich claims that bullies are often the people most hurt by bullying. Do you agree with her argument? Or do you think that the people who get bullied suffer more? Explain your answer.

Viewpoint

2

Society Does Not Encourage Bullying

Leonard Pitts, Jr.

"Kids have been bullied and ostracized from the beginning of time. Why is it they are just now picking up guns?"

Leonard Pitts Jr. is critical of the argument that bullied children are so angry and alienated after having been tormented that resorting to violence is their only option. He acknowledges that a bully can make a child miserable but he does not understand why such violent retribution seems to be the normal reaction now. Pitts contends that there is a big difference between wanting to take revenge against a bully and resorting to violence that affects not only the bully but people who were not involved in the bullying in the first place. Pitts, a columnist for the Miami Herald, wrote this article for the *Lawrence Journal-World*.

AS YOU READ, CONSIDER THE FOLLOWING QUESTIONS:
1. According to Pitts, what were the two motives of the teenagers who were planning a massacre at their high school?
2. Why does the author laugh when people tell him that he is insensitive to the problems of children who are bullied?
3. Why does the author feel that it is not right to shift the blame for a crime to the victims who have been bullied?

S ome people are going to think I'm insensitive.

I refer to the news out of the suburbs of Tacoma, Wash., that three teenagers were arrested last week for allegedly plotting a Columbine-style massacre at their high school. It is unknown how serious the alleged plan was. Authorities say the students—an 18-year-old female and two males, ages 16 and 18—had amassed no weapons and were a long way from carrying out the purported plot.

Nevertheless, the trio had allegedly filled notebooks with maps of Spanaway Lake High, along with attack plans and strategies to kill police officers who responded to the scene. The alleged plot was foiled by the father of one of the students. He became suspicious of some of his son's writings and alerted authorities. They say the students had two motives: they wanted to show that even in a time of heightened terror alerts, no place is safe from attack.

And they wanted revenge.

A young girl faces felony assault charges for accidentally injuring a boy who had been bullying her.

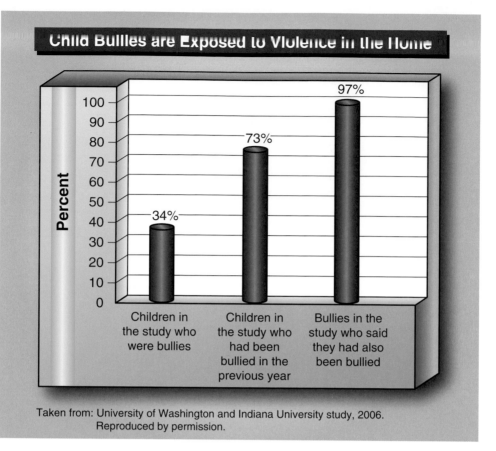

Child Bullies are Exposed to Violence in the Home

Taken from: University of Washington and Indiana University study, 2006. Reproduced by permission.

We are told the kids were angry over years of being picked on and teased. The father of one of them says his son is a small person who was bullied so regularly that he had to be escorted to the bus stop every morning.

Here's the insensitive part: So what?

We have become sadly experienced with school massacres in recent years. We have seen many disaffected loners turn campuses into killing grounds. And then comes the inevitable explanation.

He was an outcast.

He was jilted by a girl.

The other kids bullied him.

And I repeat: So what?

The last time I said that, a reader told me I obviously had no idea what it feels like to be teased and bullied in school. That one made me laugh.

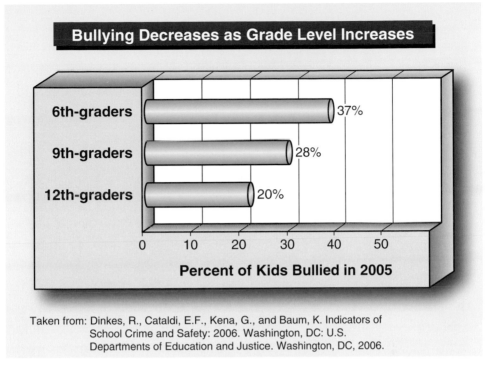

Bullying Decreases as Grade Level Increases

6th-graders 37%

9th-graders 28%

12th-graders 20%

0 10 20 30 40 50

Percent of Kids Bullied in 2005

Taken from: Dinkes, R., Cataldi, E.F., Kena, G., and Baum, K. Indicators of School Crime and Safety: 2006. Washington, DC: U.S. Departments of Education and Justice. Washington, DC, 2006.

I still have old pairs of glasses with cracked lenses, the black plastic frames held together by tape because some schoolyard tyrant decided to work out his aggressions on my face. My wife, whom I've known since fifth grade, once had to run and get my folks after some boys jacked me up and tried to inject me with hypodermic needles they'd found in the trash behind a medical clinic.

So yeah, I know a little something about being bullied. And yeah, too, I know something about wanting to mash the face of some jerk who'd made my days miserable.

There is, however, a gulf of difference between wanting to do that and wanting to indiscriminately massacre a schoolyard full of people. It takes a special kind of arrogance, self-absorption and entitlement to believe that your humiliation and pain merit the lives of a dozen strangers.

Of course, entitlement, self-absorption and arrogance are the unavoidable byproduct of a culture that teaches that shame is a four letter word, boundaries are obsolete and self-gratification is life's highest purpose.

I'm not blind. I know that bullies turn classrooms into torture chambers. I know that adolescence is a time when emotions run hot and one does not always have the perspective to understand that even the worst ordeal eventually passes away.

But I also know there is nothing new about any of that.

What's changed, then, is not the situation, but the way many young people respond to it. The way they seem to take each torment as a personal affront, an insult not to be borne on pain of death.

So to say a child killed people because he was bullied or ostracized is to dignify the act with false rationality—and to shift the onus for the crime to its victims. I get impatient with hearing that because it explains everything and explains nothing, because it does not help me understand how a child can become so alienated from his own humanity and finally, because it does not address, much less answer, a question that ought be painfully obvious.

Kids have been bullied and ostracized from the beginning of time. Why is it they are just now picking up guns?

EVALUATING THE AUTHOR'S ARGUMENTS:

In the viewpoint you just read, Leonard Pitts Jr., does not understand how a bullied child can forget that he is human and focus on taking revenge on his tormentors and others as well. Why do you think this happens?

Viewpoint

3

Video Games Contribute to Bullying and Violence

Barbara Meltz

"Because it's torn from a teen's real life, it becomes a how-to manual."

In the following viewpoint, Barbara Meltz examines the controversy over whether video games, in general, and a new game entitled "Bully," in particular, might encourage children to become violent. According to opponents, children playing this game will learn that the only way to solve a problem is through violence. In the video, the bullied teenager retaliates against his tormentors with increasing violence, which makes opponents afraid that bullied children in real life will react in the same manner to those bullying them. Barbara Meltz is a reporter for *The Boston Globe*, which published this article.

AS YOU READ, CONSIDER THE FOLLOWING QUESTIONS:

1. According to Barbara Coloroso in this viewpoint, what is the one redeeming quality of "Bully"?
2. What is a currently held belief about bully prevention?
3. According to Meltz, why does Izzy Kalman recommend this game?

A new video game that deals with a class bully is reigniting the controversy over school violence and drawing heated criticism from bullying prevention experts who say the game could embolden teen players to use aggression.

The National Institute on Media and the Family is telling parents to beware and urging retailers not to sell the game Bully to teens. An international bullying prevention program at Clemson University in South Carolina is encouraging boycotts. In Britain, three major electronic retailers say they won't stock it.

FAST FACT

The Entertainment Software Rating Board uses the following ratings for video games: EC (Early Childhood), kids three years old and older; E (Everyone), six years old and older; E10+ (Everyone +10), ten and older; T (Teen), thirteen and older; M (Mature), seventeen and older; AO (Adults Only), eighteen and older; and RP (rating pending).

"We don't think this game is appropriate for kids of any age," said psychologist Dave Walsh, president of the National Institute on Media and the Family, where a staffer played for nine of the 40 hours it takes to play Bully. "It glamorizes and rewards the kind of anti social behaviors that teachers struggle with every day."

The game does not include guns, blood, or gore. Critics say it is violent nonetheless.

"In one scene, the so-called hero sits in a tree like a sniper," said Walsh. "Instead of a firearm, he has a slingshot. His target is the football team."

Jack Thompson, a Miami attorney who represented the parents of three girls who were killed by a classmate in a 1997 school shooting in Paducah, Ky., tried unsuccessfully to block sales of Bully in Florida. "If anything, the sanitation of violence makes it more dangerous," he said in an interview. "You see no consequences for your actions other than your victory. . . . It is predictable that this will produce copy catting in schools around the country."

The company behind Bully, Rockstar Games, has seen controversy before. It produced Grand Theft Auto: San Andreas, which Wal-Mart refused to sell because of its violence and which Rockstar recalled last

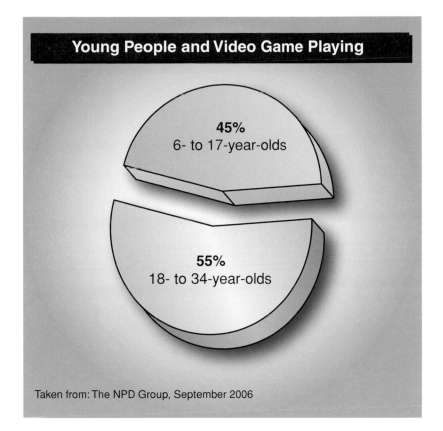

Young People and Video Game Playing

45%
6- to 17-year-olds

55%
18- to 34-year-olds

Taken from: The NPD Group, September 2006

year after it was discovered to contain a hidden scene of graphic sex. Rockstar spokesman Rodney Walker was not forthcoming in an interview when asked to discuss Bully. "I don't understand your question," he said several times when asked about the game's content.

In a subsequent e-mail, he wrote: "We'll never convince everyone, but we hope people will enjoy the story in Bully as much as they enjoy similar stories in books, plays, and movies."

Bully centers on Jimmy Hopkins, the new kid at a reform school. When he sees nerds being bullied, he decides to help them.

"We encourage bystanders to do that," said Barbara Coloroso, author of "The Bully, the Bullied, and the Bystander." Unfortunately, she added, "that's where the redeeming qualities end." What ensues is a series of escalating acts of aggression that Coloroso said "legitimize violence as a solution to a problem."

When the game was released Tuesday, her 29-year-old son, Joe, and a friend began to play. While they both said it was "cool in a Grand Theft Auto kind of way," Joe said some content is questionable. "You run into a gym teacher at a porn shop," he said. "You take over cliques by whomping them. You beat up a homeless man." Even when Jimmy gets a good grade on a chemistry test, his reward enables aggression: He gets firecrackers and stink bombs to use against the bullies.

"This is an example of the inadequacy of the rating system," said Walsh, referring to the voluntary ratings from the Entertainment Software Rating Board. Bully is rated T, for teens 13 and older. Walsh would prefer an M (mature) rating, for 17 and older.

Thompson is trying to get the rating board to do just that. In a forceful letter Thursday to the board, he argues that an M rating is warranted because of what he learned from a college student who this week managed to play most of the game and discovered that, in its later stages, the player can beat up girls and school faculty, and even throw explosive devices, with little consequence. The game teaches children to engage in "bully-back vendettas," he writes: "Every bullying expert in the world knows that this is a recipe for disaster, a recipe for Columbine." [A school shooting that took place on April 20, 1999, in Littleton, Co.]

What troubles educator Marlene Snyder, national training coordinator for the Olweus Bullying Prevention Program at Clemson, is that Bully is set in a high school rather than in a fantastical setting and that it deals with relationships rather than with inanimate objects such as cars.

"Because it's torn from a teen's real life, it becomes a how-to manual," she says. "In a world of escalating violence, this is not the message we need to be giving kids."

The current practice in bully prevention is to empower bystanders, but the idea is to marginalize a bully rather than resort to his tactics.

"The first thing to do is change the climate in a classroom or school, so everyone knows what specific aggressive behaviors are not OK—for instance, 'In this class, we don't call people names,'" says sociologist David Finkelhor, director of the Crimes Against Children Research Center at the University of New Hampshire.

Classmates need to learn how to show disapproval and when to get adult help, and adults need to know how to intervene. "A lot of bullying happens because adults allow it to with their silence," says Nancy Mullin of the Wellesley Centers for Women, co author of the "Quit It!" anti-bullying curriculum.

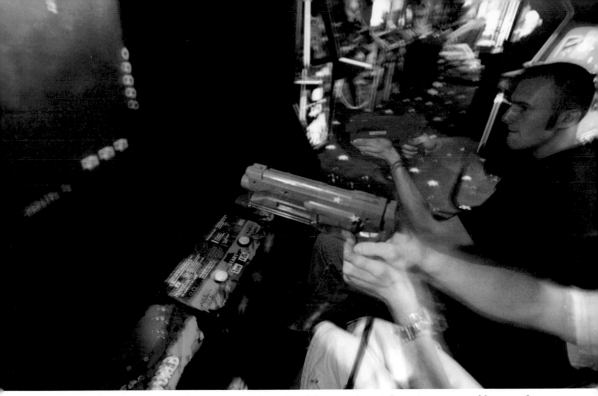

Many believe that violent video games teach adolescents that violence is an acceptable way of solving problems.

What's particularly sad, says Coloroso, is that most teen players will have had some kind of real-life experience with bullying.

"For a young kid who's been relentlessly tormented, afraid to go to school, socially isolated, the game provides a kind of comfort: 'Yes! This guy gets back at them!' "she says. Even if it doesn't incite that teen to aggression—which video games may have done in the case of the high school shootings at Columbine and elsewhere—she says, "The more they play, the more the neural pathways in the brain connect violence to pleasure."

At least one school psychologist has no problem with Bully, which he played for about an hour. The self-published author of "Bullies to Buddies" and an acknowledged fan of violent games, Izzy Kalman of Staten Island says he was invited to preview Bully. "I am comfortable recommending the game," he said. "If it incites aggression, I'm pretty sure it would be play fighting."

Doug Gentile, a developmental psychologist at Iowa State University doesn't buy it.

"Study after study since the 1960s shows that there's nothing wrong with seeing violence if what you learn is that violence is bad," he says. "But if it's just that the good guy is better at violence than the bad guy, that's a problem."

That gets to the other problem with Bully," says Joe Coloroso: "You sometimes have the chance to choose nonviolence. But then you lose."

EVALUATING THE AUTHOR'S ARGUMENTS:

In the viewpoint you just read, opponents of "Bully" argue that the video game teaches children to retaliate with violence against bullies, rather than reaching out to adults for help. Do you agree with this argument? If you have played video games similar to "Bully," do you feel they encourage you to be more violent? If so, why?

Video Game Violence Does Not Contribute to Bullying

Paul K. McMasters

". . . 'Bully' did contain some violence but 'less than we see on television every night.'"

In the following viewpoint, Paul K. McMasters argues that the uproar over the Bully video game is unnecessary because crime statistics do not show a connection between media violence and violence among young people. He agrees that society should be concerned about the effects of media violence on children, but maintains that allowing material to be censored is not the answer; rather, he believes that parents, character-building education programs in schools, and greater media responsibility is more appropriate. Paul K. McMasters, who is First Amendment ombudsman at the First Amendment Center in Arlington, Virginia, wrote this article for *The Daily Record* in Baltimore, Maryland.

AS YOU READ, CONSIDER THE FOLLOWING QUESTIONS:
1. For which ages is "Bully" rated, according to McMasters?
2. In the opinion of the author, besides video games, what other two media are considered to be threats to America's youth?

In May 2005, video-game developer Rockstar Games, publisher of the controversial "Grand Theft Auto" series, announced that this October it would release a new game called "Bully." The one-sentence announcement merely said that the game, rated for players 13 years and older, featured "a troublesome schoolboy" confronting the problems of being dumped at a fictitious reform school.

But that was enough to send battalions of activists and others into a panic.

School boards around the nation banned the game. Young demonstrators gathered outside Rockstar's headquarters in New York. CNN's Lou Dobbs warned his viewers that "Bully" was "another example of our culture in decline." Across the waters, the British House of Commons condemned the company that produced it and stores banned it from their shelves. And, of course, there was lots of ominous coverage and commentary in the media.

All this occurred, mind you, before the video game was seen, let alone put on the market.

In fact, "Bully" appears to be a lot tamer than a lot of other gaming fare. Clive Thompson, who reviewed it on Wired.com earlier this month, wrote that "The game doesn't glorify bullying at all. Indeed, it's almost precisely the opposite."

But before its contents were actually known, Miami lawyer Jack Thompson, who campaigns against pornography and rap music as well as video games, had persuaded a Florida judge to order a demonstration of the game in court. On Oct. 13, [2006] Judge Ronald

FAST FACT

According to the Entertainment Software Association and the NPD Group, 49 percent of computer and video games sold in 2005 were rated E (Everyone); 4 percent were rated E10+ (Everyone 10 years and older); 32 percent were rated T (Teens thirteen and older); and 15 percent were rated M (Mature seventeen and older).

Students write compliments on each other's backs as part of the Peace Builder's program designed to turn bullies into better classroom citizens.

Friedman ruled that the game did not qualify as a "public nuisance" under the pollution law invoked in Thompson's lawsuit and allowed the game's release. The judge noted in court that "Bully" did contain some violence but "less than we see on television every night."

Ironically, Judge Friedman's decision came one day after a federal judge in Oklahoma blocked enforcement of a new state law prohibiting the sale of violent video games to children—the latest in a lengthening list of similar decisions across the nation.

Video games, it appears, are replacing television, which replaced movies, which replaced the penny press, as the "new pornography" threatening the minds and morals of the nation's youth.

For more than eight decades, dating to the Payne Fund studies on movie violence in 1933, experts have produced study after study and political leaders have conducted hearing after hearing, all in an effort to prove—by repetition if not by hard evidence— that media violence harms young people, even adults.

Despite those efforts, drawing a straight line from violence in the media to violence in reality remains difficult if not impossible. The cause-and-effect relationship cannot be produced reliably in the lab nor demonstrated plausibly in real life. Common experience, common sense and logic also get in the way.

In fact, hard evidence in the form of crime statistics goes in the other direction. Although there has been a steady—and to some an alarming—increase in fictional violence in electronic media over recent decades, that has been accompanied by a steady decline in the violent-crime rate. The number of violent crimes per 100,000 people has gone from a high in 1990 of 729.6 to 469.2 in 2005.

Statistics for juveniles are even more dramatic. Juvenile arrest rates for all crimes decreased by 31 percent between 1996 and 2004. According to the Violent Crime Index maintained by the FBI, the violent-crime arrest rate among 10- to 17-year-olds for 2004 was lower than in any year since 1980—and 49 percent below the peak year of 1994.

While young people and adults have been exposed to larger and larger doses of fictional violence in more kinds of media, the actual

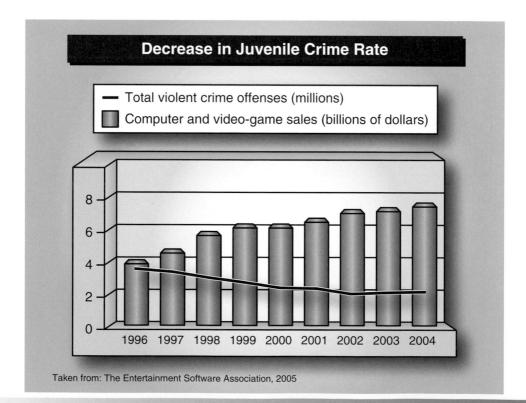

Decrease in Juvenile Crime Rate

— Total violent crime offenses (millions)

▨ Computer and video-game sales (billions of dollars)

1996 1997 1998 1999 2000 2001 2002 2003 2004

Taken from: The Entertainment Software Association, 2005

violent crime that exposure is supposed to foment has not material-
ized. Just the opposite.

Parents instinctively want to protect their children from actual
violence. It is certainly understandable that they would worry about
the effects of media violence on their children also. They are free to
act on those legitimate concerns.

More parental involvement, along with character building in school
and responsibility on the part of the media, indeed, are the appropriate ways to address concerns raised by violent media. But delegating
that job to legislators, judges and would-be censors driven by fear and
hunches is unwise, ineffective and, ultimately, unconstitutional.

EVALUATING THE AUTHOR'S ARGUMENTS:

In this viewpoint, Paul K. McMasters uses statistics to
make his point that media violence does not contribute
to youth violence. Do you find his argument persuasive?
Why or why not?

Children Learn to Bully from Parents

Kim Schafer

"A mom or dad who consistently uses aggressive language or behaviors might have a little bully in the making."

In the following viewpoint, Kim Schafer contends that children learn their behavior from their parents, and children whose parents are bullies are more likely to become bullies themselves. Children often become bullies after having witnessed their parents bullying others and after having been bullied themselves. She argues that it is unfair to assume that adult bullies are poor and uneducated. Schafer maintains that the children of bullies are forced into a cycle in which bullying becomes a way of life. Kim Schafer, a family therapist, wrote this article for *Inside SCV.*

AS YOU READ, CONSIDER THE FOLLOWING QUESTIONS:
1. What might cause a child to become a bully, according to the author?
2. In the author's opinion, what two things do children who bully want?
3. According to the author, what are the four different kinds of bullies?

Webster defines "bully" as "one who is habitually cruel or abusive to others," and defines "habitually" as "a mode of behavior that has become nearly or completely involuntary." In other words, bullying is an action done so often that one may not even realize they're doing it.

A child may become a bully when they grow up with an aggressive model that is consistently repetitive. Too often in a child's life that model is their parent. A mom or dad who consistently uses aggressive language or behaviors might have a little bully in the making. As a parent, the choices you make and the actions you take can change your children's lives.

Sometimes bullying is subtle; maybe mom is consistently rude to the bank teller, the teacher, the clerk at the grocery store or the teenager taking orders in the drive-thru window. Maybe dad has trouble with road rage and a habit of letting loose with verbal epitaphs while the kids are riding in the car with him.

Parents who bully were kids who never learned how to control their own anger. Parents who bully often support their child's aggressive behaviors. They also often use bullying as a method of controlling their kids or "toughening them up."

Bullying Knows No Bounds

Bullying knows no financial, cultural or social bounds. It's a mistake to think that an adult bully only lives on the poor side of town, drinks too much and never graduated high school. They may be extremely educated, have a professional career and be influential in their community. Bullying doesn't always look the same but it has the same devastating effect on everyone.

> **FAST FACT**
>
> According to a University of Washington and Indiana University study, 97 percent of the children in the study who bullied others had been bullied themselves.

During adolescence, bullying is not a problem that usually sorts itself out—especially if there is a parent who bullies lurking in the background. When a child is repeatedly victimized by a parent who uses bullying as a coping strategy, behaviors and attitudes tend to emerge

It has been suggested that children who see their parents using aggressive behavior with others may in turn become bullies themselves.

which are inconsistent with the child's natural personality. These kids tend to take on the attitude modeled by the parent and act it out in their peer environment. Children who bully are seeking to gain control and power. The goal is to put a victim in some type of distress. When children are bullied by their parents they in turn may bully their peers to gain control over some portion of their life. Children who bully desire to dominate their peers. They need to win. They often have no remorse and usually refuse to accept responsibility. Ironically, their parents usually defend these behaviors when parent and child are confronted by school administration or a peer's parents.

Just like the wide variety of bullying behaviors represented in adults, children express their need to gain power and control in a myriad of ways. Studies on bullying break down the kinds of bullies into physical, verbal, relational and reactive. Children who use physical methods of bullying are action-oriented and need to hurt their victim or their victim's property. These children may have witnessed their parent's frequent use of physical force or they themselves are the victims of physical abuse.

Verbal bullies use words to hurt or humiliate another person. These children may be at the mercy of their parent's insulting, demeaning comments or they may have grown up listening to mom and dad verbally bully other adults to get what they want.

Reactive victims are victims who have been bullied, react impulsively, fight back and become a bully in retaliation. This type of bully may be the child always picked on at home by parents or older siblings.

The effects of bullying last a lifetime. Unless children are taught how to use new behaviors they may grow up to bully their spouses, their children and even their co-workers. How do you teach these children to break the generational cycle they've been exposed to? To begin to tackle the problem it takes teachers, support staff, administrators and other family members and friends to join together and take action against bullying.

EVALUATING THE AUTHOR'S ARGUMENTS:

In the viewpoint you just read, Kim Schafer maintains that children learn to be bullies from watching their parents. Do you find her arguments persuasive? Who else might influence children's behavior?

Viewpoint

6

Children Learn to Bully from Television

Maggie McKee

"Four-year-olds who watched the average amount of television— 3.5 hours per day— were 25% more likely to become bullies than those who watched none.

In the following viewpoint, Maggie McKee, a writer for *New Scientist* magazine, discusses how watching violent cartoons can cause children as young as four to become bullies. She examines studies that show the connection between violence in cartoons (even G-rated cartoons) and bullying and aggressive behavior, and how parents can positively influence their children's behavior with emotional support and attention.

AS YOU READ, CONSIDER THE FOLLOWING QUESTIONS:
1. According to the author, how much television do four-year-olds have to watch to become 200 percent more likely to become bullies?
2. According to this viewpoint, besides bullying, what are other negative effects of watching too much television?
3. What kinds of things can parents do to help reduce bullying in their kids?

Some studies have shown that young children who watch a lot of television, especially violent animated shows, are more likely to become desensitized to violence.

Young children who watch a lot of television are more likely to become bullies, a new study reveals. The authors suggest the increasingly violent nature of children's cartoons may be to blame.

Previous studies have linked television to aggressive behaviour in older children and adolescents. But a team led by Frederick Zimmerman, an economist at the University of Washington in Seattle, US, has now traced the phenomenon to four-year-olds.

More TV, More Violent

The researchers used existing data from a national US survey to study the amount of television watched by 1,266 four-year-olds. Then they compared that amount with follow-up reports—by the children's mothers—on whether the children bullied or were "cruel or mean to others" when they were between six and 11 years old.

The study showed that four-year-olds who watched the average amount of television—3.5 hours per day—were 25% more likely to become bullies than those who watched none. And children who watched eight hours of television a day were 200% more likely to become bullies.

Effect of TV Violence on Children

How much, if at all, do you think exposure to violence in TV shows contributes to violent behavior in children? Does it contribute . . .

	Current	6/01
A lot	44	47
Somewhat	37	32
Only a little	14	14
Not at all	5	6
Don't know/Refused	1	2

Taken from: "Parents, Media and Public Policy," The Henry J. Kaiser Family Foundation, 2004. Reproduced by permission.

Violence Becomes a Fact of Life

The study did not probe what types of programmes the children were watching, but Zimmerman suggests they were mainly animated videos and cartoons. He says such shows may follow a trend seen in movies and cites a recent study showing the average G-rated kids' movie contains (U-rated in the UK) about 9.5 minutes of violence—up from 6 minutes in 1940.

"What I suspect is these violent animated shows are causing kids to become desensitised to violence," he told *New Scientist*. "Parents should understand that, just because a TV show or movie is made for kids, it doesn't mean it's good for kids—especially four-year-olds."

He suggests parents follow guidelines set by the American Academy of Pediatrics, which recommends no television for children under two and no more than two hours a day for older kids. "We have added bullying to the list of potential negative consequences of excessive television viewing, along with obesity, inattention, and other types of aggression," write the authors in the *Archives of Pediatrics & Adolescent Medicine*.

Parents Can Make a Difference

The study also looked at two other factors thought to decrease the likelihood of bullying—cognitive stimulation and parental emotional support. It found that children whose parents regularly exposed them to ideas—by reading aloud or taking them to museums, for example—were a third less likely to become bullies, as were those whose parents provided them with emotional support—by eating meals together and talking.

"Each of these things has an independent effect," says Zimmerman. "So parents who are not going to read to their children and who put their kids in front of the TV instead [represent] a double whammy" for their children's chances of becoming bullies, he says.

Some would argue that parents of children genetically predisposed to bad behaviours and bullying may simply be putting them in front of the TV to reduce the stress of dealing with this negative behaviour, rather than the TV itself being a causal factor.

But because the effects of cognitive stimulation, emotional support and television viewing can be teased apart and examined separately, Zimmerman says the chances of the bad behaviours coming before the excess TV viewing are generally reduced.

EVALUATING THE AUTHOR'S ARGUMENTS:

In the viewpoint you just read, the author cites several studies that found that watching a lot of violent cartoons can lead to bullying and aggressive behavior. Do you feel that watching a violent cartoon has the same effect on a child as a live-action movie or TV show? Why or why not?

Chapter 2

How Can Parents and Others Combat Bullying?

Parents and schools are exploring the best ways to protect their children from bullying.

Viewpoint

1

Changes in Society Can Prevent School Bullying

Thomas Brown

In the following viewpoint, Thomas Brown is critical of Americans who seem to be more concerned with the every day and mundane details of life instead of trying to solve the problems that bullied children face every day. Brown argues that bullied children commit suicide and kill their classmates because they feel that no one is interested enough to help them. Thomas Brown wrote this article for Bully Police USA, a Web site devoted to helping bullied children, and he is the creator of the Broken Toy Project, which began as a movie about a bullied child and his tormentors, and which Brown uses as the basis for workshops at schools to present a picture of the problems children suffer at the hands of bullies.

"And they kill classmates . . . these 'teased' and 'bullied' kids."

AS YOU READ, CONSIDER THE FOLLOWING QUESTIONS:
1. According to the author, what does bullying drive some children to do?
2. In the author's opinion, who's at fault for not helping kids who are bullied?
3. Why can't children who are bullied concentrate on and excel in their class work, in the author's opinion?

I t's just about dawn here on the 22nd of March [2005]. Another day in this great land of ours has begun. For some it will be another day of work and the occasional daily ritual of gathering around the water-cooler at work or in chairs at barbershops, talking about the news that really matters.

I can hear it now.

"Will the King of Pop [Michael Jackson] make it on-time to court today?" "I wonder what the judge will rule in the [Terri] Schiavo case?" "Do you think Barry Bonds is telling the truth about steroids?" "Did you see [Jay] Leno last night? Damn, that guy is funny!" "I'll bet a dime to a doughnut that Robert Blake did it." "My kids loved Robots." "I've got to rush out after work and get Scottie another pair of soccer shorts. He's so hard on them."

> **FAST FACT**
>
> More than 5.7 million teens (almost 30 percent) in the United States are estimated to be a bully, a target of bullying, or both.

And in some places the conversation might be . . .

"Some friggin' kid blew away a bunch of school kids in Minnesota." "I heard he was an Indian." "I don't care what the hell he was, put em' in the chair. If they're old enough to kill, then they're old enough to die for their crime." "That [Bill] O'Reilly is right as usual." "If you ask me, it's time to get prayer back in schools." "If you ask me, it's time to bring back the board." "Kids these days just don't respect anyone." "I hope they fry the little bastard."

That won't be possible. Young Jeff Weise killed himself before authorities could get to him. Reports are now coming in that Jeff laughed a lot while he pulled the trigger and students are saying that they could hear cries of "No, Jeff, no!" and "Why?"

And just like it has happened so many times before following a school shooting, at least one person interviewed by the authorities or the media is saying that the shooter was teased by classmates. . . .

Bullying Should Not Be a Part of Life

Teased . . . harassed . . . picked on . . . bullied. It's all the same.

So what.

Everyone gets teased and bullied now and then. Bullying is a part of life . . . it's part of being a kid.

It makes you tougher.

Bullcrap.

Yep . . . that's what I just said . . . and that's exactly what I mean.

Just how many school shootings "is" it going to take before we finally wake up in this great land of ours and face the brutal reality that many of our schools are simply not safe?

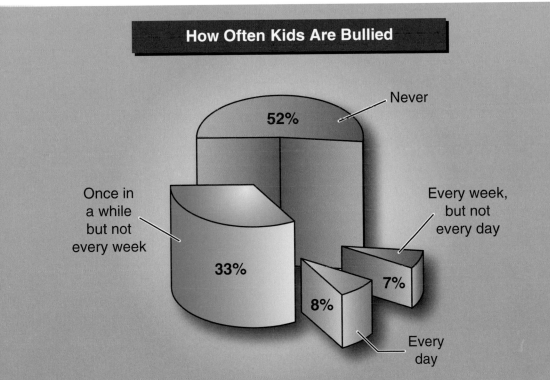

How Often Kids Are Bullied

52% — Never

Once in a while but not every week — 33%

8% — Every day

Every week, but not every day — 7%

Taken from: Kids Health, March 2004

Bullied Children Commit Suicide

Just how many times "do" we have to hear about a bullied child taking their own life, simply because they can't bear another day of emotional and physical torture in their school, before we get off our butts and do something about this problem?

They hang themselves with a lamp cord . . . they overdose on pills . . . they shoot themselves in the head . . . they throw themselves in front of trains . . .

And they kill classmates. . .

. . . these "teased" and "bullied" kids.

Kevin Epling, whose teenage son committed suicide after being bullied, speaks at a rally in Michigan supporting legislation requiring schools to adopt anti-bullying policies.

There are a handful of states that have done the right thing for our kids. They have put laws into place about bullying. There are some states that are "considering" putting laws into place about bullying. In my mind there shouldn't be any "considering." It's a no-brainer. It should be a done deal.

Antibullying Laws Are Needed

But the majority of the states in this country seem to care more about standardized and proficiency tests in our schools . . . than the safety and security of the school kids that take those tests in the first place.

I ask you. Just how proficient can we expect children to "be" if, while they're sitting in their chair taking that test, their mind is only on the daily bullying they endure in their school?

For that child already knows, that whether it be in the lunch room, or in the hallway, or in the bathroom, or on the playground, or during gym, or in the locker room, or on the bus, at least one person is going to add to their misery. . . . At least one child will become the center of attention as they "tease" and "bully" while dozens of other children stand around and do absolutely nothing but watch.

Bullied Kids Are Pushed Toward Violence

Perhaps that child is thinking about ending their pain once and for all, thinking about that big rope in Grandpa's barn, or those sleeping pills in the medicine cabinet. Or, perhaps that child is thinking about the big gun in Uncle Fred's homemade cabinet.

Perhaps that child is thinking about getting even with the bullies . . . with the kids that stand around and do nothing . . . with the teacher who tells him to quit tattling . . . with the Principal who ignores his cries of desperation and for help.

America, I guarantee that while you're reading this those thoughts are going through some kids' minds; more kids than we can imagine.

Kids Should Matter More

At one time those same thoughts were in the mind of the boy in Minnesota who gunned down classmates, as it has been in the minds of the school shooters at Columbine, in Springfield Oregon, in West Paducah Kentucky, in Pearl Mississippi and several other places throughout the planet.

And, by God, that should matter to us.
As much as feeding tubes . . . and Michael Jackson . . . and steroids .
. . and Scottie's soccer pants.
It really "should" matter.

EVALUATING THE AUTHOR'S ARGUMENTS:

In the viewpoint you just read, Thomas Brown disagrees with the idea that bullying should be regarded as "a part of life," in which every child is, at some point, picked on, and in which each child must learn to deal with it. He feels that bullying contributes to the number of children who commit suicide and the number of children who bring guns to school and kill their classmates. Do you agree with Brown? Why or why not?

Viewpoint 2

Homeschooling Can Help Prevent School Bullying

Susan Wight

"Bullying is an inevitable part of school culture and children are better off home educated."

In the following viewpoint, Susan Wight defends the idea of educating children at home in order both to protect them from bullies and to prepare them better to deal with bullies as adults. She rejects the idea that children who are homeschooled are somehow at a disadvantage because they are not being taught how to cope with bullies and the real world; rather, she maintains that children who are bullied at school are not being helped because the school system does not truly address or solve their problems. Susan Wight is a coeditor of *Otherways* magazine, which is published by the Home Education Network.

AS YOU READ, CONSIDER THE FOLLOWING QUESTIONS:

1. According to the author, how old was Marie Bentham when she committed suicide?
2. What percentage of bullying is observed by teachers, according to a Canadian study cited by the author?

During the holidays Marie Bentham cried as she told her family about being bullied at school. Her concerned mother had already contacted the school which had followed its bullying policy and fully investigated the incidents. The bullying had continued. The day before school resumed, Marie refused to go back. Her mother was unsure how to deal with the situation and sent her to bed, convinced that children must go to school. Eight-year-old Marie Bentham strangled herself with her skipping rope that night—it was her only way to ensure she would never have to face those bullies again.

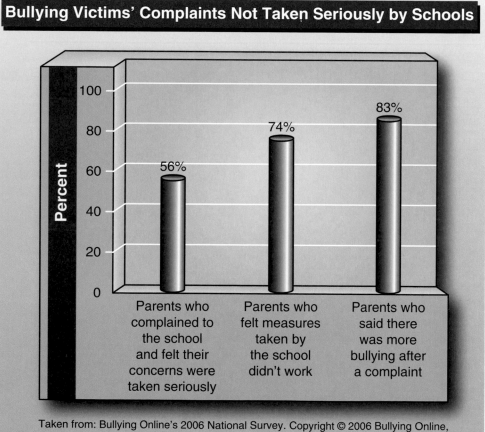

Bullying Victims' Complaints Not Taken Seriously by Schools

Taken from: Bullying Online's 2006 National Survey. Copyright © 2006 Bullying Online, www.bullying.co.uk. Reproduced by permission.

Marie Bentham is the youngest recorded suicide connected with bullying, but far from the only one. These suggest there is no safe level of bullying, but victims bullied for a year or more are six times more likely to contemplate or commit suicide and four times more likely to suffer lifelong lack of self-esteem. A survey of over 1,000 adults showed school bullying not only affects people's self-esteem, but also their ability to make friends, succeed in education and in work and in social relationships. Bullying also results in anxiety, headaches, nausea, ulcers, sleeplessness, lack of confidence, isolation, depression, post-traumatic stress disorder, flashes of anger and hostility.

Bullying Leaves Long-Lasting Effects

Bullying may be verbal, physical, psychological, sexual or consist of ostracism. It occurs in the play-ground, the classroom and on the way to and from school. Physical injuries have included bruises, black eyes, broken bones, inter-nal injuries, scarring, damaged testicles and kidneys, and being blinded in one eye. Bullying activity has included stabbings, severe beatings, being strung upside down in toilets and almost drowning, being thrown down cliffs into water and pushed onto the road in front of oncoming traffic to being raped or having objects inserted into various orifices and almost killed. Bullying understandably increases anxiety and depression, decreases learning abilities and causes lowered immunity.

> **FAST FACT**
>
> Approximately 1.1 million children were being home-schooled in 2003, according to a National Center for Education Statistics report.

Bullied children wake knowing bullies are waiting to torment, humiliate and hurt them. Some people believe bullying teaches chil-dren to stand up for themselves. On the contrary, bullying is destruc-tive, humiliating and abusive.

School policies cannot prevent bullying. Most bullying is not reported to, or noticed by, teachers. A Canadian study videotaped children playing in a schoolyard and found teachers were aware of only 17 per cent of the bullying observed by the researchers.

Some people believe that a nurturing home-school experience may provide children with a better chance to develop strong self-esteem and learn positive conflict-resolution skills from their parents.

Schools Cannot Prevent Bullying

Even when schools are aware of bullying and follow their bullying policies, there is no guarantee it will stop. In Marie Bentham's case the school reportedly took the complaints "very seriously", "investigated them fully" and "dealt with them promptly". The local council investigating Marie's bullying said, "There was nothing to raise any serious concerns". When these words were written, Marie was already dead.

Although officially condemned, bullying is an unavoidable fact of school life. Australian bullying expert Dr. Ken Rigby has found 50 per cent of Australian school children have experienced bullying and one in six is bullied weekly. It has always been a problem in schools.

Sometimes teachers quell obvious bullying but do not notice more devious bullying. Schools claiming to have no bullying are regarded by researchers as "bullying black-spots". Australian expert Evelyn Field believes "under optimal conditions bullying can be reduced by up to 50 percent" but that it "cannot be eradicated".

Kids Cannot Be Taught to Be Bully-Proof

Many anti-bullying books urge parents to teach their children self-respect, assertive skills and how to make friends to "bully-proof" themselves, but these skills are difficult to achieve, especially for children already stressed by bullying. As researcher Keith Sullivan points out, "To suggest that people . . . being bullied should stand up for themselves is not only unfair, it is also unrealistic. If they could have stood up for themselves, they would not have been bullied and the bullying undermines any vestiges of strength they had".

Children need to learn skills to enable them to cope with bullies in later life, and home education provides a much more respectful environment to learn them. Children absorb values, beliefs and morals from those around them. They can learn these more effectively in the safe environment of home and naturally widening social circle as they get older. Ideally their parents will model assertive behaviour and conflict resolution skills and family relationships will inevitably offer endless opportunities to practice them. Children can learn to confidently communicate and stand up for their point of view in a supportive and safe environment.

Home Education Provides a Safer Environment

Some experts claim bullied children tend to come from families where parents are not assertive. They might argue that home education would only compound their problems by protecting them from exposure to bullying behaviour at school, leaving them unable to defend themselves from bullies as adults. It seems an odd solution to condemn children to years of abuse and its long-term effects so they can learn to deal with it. Moreover, the Kidscape survey concluded that, "contrary to popular opinion, bullying does not help children to cope better with adult life. In fact it has the opposite effect".

Bullying, together with school violence, is now a major reason for choosing to home educate. Sadly many parents who know about home education have been brainwashed to believe children must go to school. However, families are now showing their capacity to see the truth. Bullying is an inevitable part of school culture and children are better off home educated.

EVALUATING THE AUTHOR'S ARGUMENTS:

In the viewpoint you just read, Susan Wight contends that home education more effectively prepares a child to deal with life, in general, and bullying, in particular. Do you feel her arguments are persuasive? Why or why not? Do you feel that protecting children from exposure to bullies is an effective way to prepare them for life?

Viewpoint

3

Parents Are Responsible for the Aftermath of Bullying

Joye Brown

"It's the parents who should be making sure their children know how to treat one another."

In the following viewpoint, Joye Brown writes about the plight of a bullied child and discusses who might be more to blame—the bully's parents or the school officials. One school administrator places the blame squarely with the parents of the bully. He believes it is impossible for schools to monitor every aspect of each child's school day. This official also is critical of parents whom he feels do not bring their children up properly, and refuse to acknowledge that their children might misbehave. Joye Brown is a columnist for *Newsday*, in which this article was published.

AS YOU READ, CONSIDER THE FOLLOWING QUESTIONS:
1. According to the author, what was the response of the bully's parent after the victim punched him in the third grade?
2. In this viewpoint, what was the reaction of another mother whose son bullied the victim in fourth grade?
3. What was the reaction of the victim's mother to a lawyer's advice to call the police after each incident?

M y son is in the fifth grade," the e-mail began. "He started getting bullied in the third grade."

The mother doesn't worry about video of her son's bullying being broadcast via the Internet, like the clip of three teenagers from North Babylon beating a 13-year-old that is still making the rounds.

There is no video. But there is a photograph of the 10-year-old's bruised leg the mother shared with me. I asked to see it after exchanging e-mails and telephone calls with the mother, whose family lives in a good school district on Long Island's South Shore.

The family asked me not to publish their names, which was OK with me, because—judging from the avalanche of other bullying-related e-mails in my mailbox—they're not the only ones grappling with the scourge. To protect their privacy, I also decided not to name the school district.

For three years, their son has endured kicks, pushes, curses, even being slapped on his back by boys using cloth as a whip.

When Walking Away Doesn't Work

In third grade, the then-8-year-old followed his parents' advice: Walk away and tell someone. But that didn't work, especially during recess, when kids tackle the wilds of the school's field, while adults stake out its tamer twin, the blacktop playground.

One day, the boy decided he'd had enough. He punched his tormentor in the stomach. Mom got a call from the principal, and the boy and his bully spent a week on punishment together, swapping the freedom of recess for lunches in the principal's office. The other child's mother "called me and apologized and said, 'I am glad your son stuck up for himself. My son needed that punch,'" the mother said. "Now, there's a parent who knows her child. My son never had a problem with him again."

How Do Kids React to Bullying?

When I am bullied, I:	Percent
Tell the bully to stop	34.2
Get away from the bully	32.0
Hurt other kids	2.1
Stay home from school	3.4
Tell an adult	44.6
Tell a friend	24.0

Taken from: "What Do Children Do When They Are Bullied?" Maine Project Against Bullying, January 2000. Reproduced with permission.

In the fourth grade, a different group of kids started in on him. Mom complained to the school. She also called one child's mother.

"She basically had the 'not my son' attitude and also laughed at me," the mother said. "So now I know why he is the way he is."

Parents and Schools Not Doing Enough

Her son is now in the fifth grade. He loves football and spelling. He also loves his school, and especially, his teachers. It would be a match made in heaven—if not for continued bullying. The South Shore district takes bullying, no matter what form it takes, seriously, but that hasn't been enough to spare her son.

"He gets made fun of," the mother said. The boy defended himself

Performers from non-profit group Urban Improv interact with a fourth-grader during a workshop centering on issues like bullying, teasing, and violence.

again. And again he and the other boy were punished by the principal, as they should have been.

"I hold the school responsible, along with the parents," the mother said, "They are not doing enough." I took her family's frustration to an administrator in a different school district to get his reaction. He, too, shall remain unidentified, because I wanted his frank opinion.

"Schools know how to take care of the worst cases, but you are describing the kind of thing that goes on in schools, in buses, playgrounds, bathrooms," he said. "Schools can't police every part of the building every part of the day. From where I sit, it's the parents who should be making sure their children know how to treat one another. Parents usually want to see the best in their kids and skip over the rough spots and when they do that, we can't do much for the kind of incidents you are describing."

As for the boy's mother who wrote me, she's still trying to balance her son's loyalty to his school with his dislike of bullies. At one point, the family consulted an attorney, who said it would be difficult and expensive to fight the problem in court.

Instead, the lawyer suggested that the family call police whenever the boy got hit.

"I'm not going to do that," the mother said. "That's crazy."

Last night, the mother sat down with her son, thanking him for allowing *Newsday* to tell the family's story.

"I hope he grows to be six feet tall," she said afterward. "But he should feel that way already. If telling his story helps one kid, that would be a big thing for us and for him."

EVALUATING THE AUTHOR'S ARGUMENTS:

In the viewpoint you just read, Joye Brown quotes a school district administrator as saying that bullying occurs, in part, because, generally, parents prefer not to see any faults in their children and do nothing to curb any negative behavior. Do you feel that many parents do not want to recognize bullying behavior in their own children and might refuse to take responsibility for it? Why or why not?

Parents Are Not Responsible for the Aftermath of Bullying

Avi Salzman

" 'She absolutely should not have been charged, because it wasn't the cause of his suicide.' "

In the following viewpoint, Avi Salzman discusses the case of Judith Scruggs, a Connecticut mother who was convicted of endangering the mental health of her son, Daniel, to the point that he committed suicide because she had kept such a dirty home. The Connecticut Supreme Court overturned Scruggs' conviction, stating that it was not possible to determine when a house becomes so unclean that it could impact a child's mental health. Scruggs' lawyer argued that Daniel was more affected by the bullying he was subjected to at school than by the cleanliness of his house. Prosecutors claimed that Scruggs' neglect contributed to Daniel's suicide. Avi Salzman is a reporter for the *New York Times*.

AS YOU READ, CONSIDER THE FOLLOWING QUESTIONS:
1. According to the author, in what way was Judith Scruggs responsible for her son's suicide?
2. What is the name of the state agency that investigates suspected cases of child abuse?
3. What has Lisa Toomey's advocacy group accomplished, according to the author?

T he Connecticut Supreme Court on Monday [August 28, 2006] overturned the conviction of a woman who prosecutors said had kept such a messy home that it endangered the safety and mental health of her 12-year-old son, who killed himself in 2002. The case had sparked a national debate over parental responsibility for a child's suicide.

Blaming the Parent for a Child's Suicide

The case of Judith Scruggs, a single mother from Meriden, and her son, Daniel, was the first in which a Connecticut parent was charged

Judith Scruggs speaks to reporters after receiving a suspended sentence for creating an environment detrimental to the health of her 12-year-old son, who killed himself after being persistently bullied at school.

criminally in a child's suicide, experts said. It also brought national attention to the issue of child bullying after it was revealed that Daniel had been abused repeatedly by his classmates.

The Supreme Court ruled unanimously that prosecutors could not point to "objective standards for determining the point at which housekeeping becomes so poor that an ordinary person should know that it poses an unacceptable risk to the mental health of a child."

Justice William J. Sullivan wrote the majority opinion, and a separate concurring opinion was signed by two justices.

The ruling reversed Ms. Scruggs's conviction on one felony count of putting her child at risk by creating an unhealthy and unsafe home. She was sentenced to probation and 100 hours of community service in 2004.

Ms. Scruggs did not return messages left with her lawyer and a friend on Monday, but the friend, Lisa Toomey, said she spoke to Ms. Scruggs after the decision was released and described her as "ecstatic."

Constant Bullying Led to Suicide

During the trial, prosecutors were careful to separate the charges against Ms. Scruggs from Daniel's death, noting that they were not seeking to prove that Ms. Scruggs's conduct led to her son's suicide. Nonetheless, the trial presented a narrative of Daniel's misery, which ended on Jan. 2, 2002, when he hung himself in his bedroom closet.

> **FAST FACT**
>
> Among fifteen- to twenty-four-year-olds, suicide is the third leading cause of death and it is the sixth leading cause of death for five- to fourteen-year-olds, according to the American Academy of Child and Adolescent Psychiatry.

Witnesses testified that Daniel was punched, kicked and spat on in school and that he regularly skipped classes and even defecated in his clothes so he could be sent home.

The Scruggs home was opened up for jurors through photographs and witnesses' accounts; investigators testified that clothes, household items and debris were piled throughout the house, and that there was no clear surface in the kitchen to eat or prepare food.

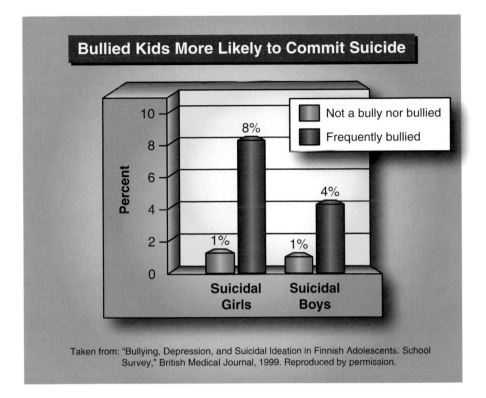

Bullied Kids More Likely to Commit Suicide

Taken from: "Bullying, Depression, and Suicidal Ideation in Finnish Adolescents: School Survey," British Medical Journal, 1999. Reproduced by permission.

Can a Messy Home Affect Mental State?

One police officer testified that the house smelled like a "dirty clothes hamper" and had "an odor of garbage." In the closet where Daniel was found, the police found a spear and three long knives.

M. H. Reese Norris, Ms. Scruggs's lawyer, argued in the trial that Daniel was far more traumatized by his experiences in school than by the mess at home.

A state report later found that Daniel had been let down by numerous agencies, including the state Department of Children and Families, which had closed an investigation into Daniel's situation just days before he died.

Ms. Scruggs is suing the Meriden school system and the city in connection with her son's death. That case is pending, lawyers said.

At her sentencing, Mr. Norris described Ms. Scruggs, who is in her mid-50's, as a struggling single parent who was working 60 hours a week at two jobs when Daniel died. The judge faulted her for failing to show remorse and for blaming her problems on others.

Place Blame on the Bullies

Douglas Nash, who represented Ms. Scruggs in her appeal, said the charges had placed blame where it did not belong.

"All you had here was a cluttered house," he said.

Ms. Toomey, a business owner from Wallingford who started an anti-bullying advocacy group after reading about Daniels suicide, said the Supreme Court's ruling showed prosecutors had "taken the attention off the root of the problem."

She said, "She absolutely should not have been charged, because it wasn't the cause of his suicide."

Hold Schools Responsible

Ms. Toomey's group worked to get legislation passed in the state legislature holding schools accountable for bullying and making it easier for students to report abuse. She said Daniel's case made parents more willing to speak out about bullying.

Lawyers and legal experts said the court's opinion would probably not shift precedent in cases in which a parent is accused of neglecting a child's needs. Still, prosecutors will be hard pressed to charge another parent whose home is unsuitable for children, said Leon F. Dalbec, who prosecuted the case.

"It's going to be difficult because of this decision," he said. "It's got to be really, really bad conditions. It's got to be so obvious that there would be no other opinion on the matter."

EVALUATING THE AUTHOR'S ARGUMENTS:

The previous viewpoint argues that some parents refuse to accept responsibility for raising children who bully others. In this viewpoint, Judith Scruggs was criticized by a judge for blaming others for her problems. Who do you feel is more at fault—parents who refuse to acknowledge that their children are bullies or someone like Judith Scruggs, who was accused of keeping such a messy home that it affected her son's mental health?

Viewpoint

5

Using the Internet to Fight Cyberbullying

Larry Kopko

"Millions of children are being cyber-bullied and many of them are not telling anyone about it."

In the following viewpoint, Larry Kopko discusses the ease with which cyberbullying can take place, and is amazed by the number of children affected by it, as well as by the large number of kids who do not tell anyone that they're being bullied. He notes that twice as many children are cyberbullied as they are bullied in person. He writes about the need for taking cyberbullying seriously, and calls on Congress to pass a bullying prevention bill. Larry Kopko, a sheriff in Warren County, Pennsylvania, wrote this article for *Sheriff* magazine, which is published by the National Sheriffs' Association.

AS YOU READ, CONSIDER THE FOLLOWING QUESTIONS:
1. What is cyberbullying, according to the author?
2. According to Fight Crime: Invest in Kids, how many children between the ages of six and seventeen are being cyberbullied?
3. In the opinion of the author, what are some of the signs that a child is a victim of cyberbullying?

Ryan Halligan was smart with two loving and supportive parents. But he harbored a secret that bullies were instant messaging him. They harassed him for months. When Ryan despaired and suggested in one online conversation that he commit suicide, a bully wrote back "Its about time." Ryan didn't tell his parents. At age 13, Ryan took his own life, a victim of cyberbullying. His father discovered the conversations only after his child's death.

Cyberbullying Can Happen Anytime

This month [September 2006] as America's kids go back to school, a new threat awaits them in hallways, computer labs and in the playground—cyberbullying. Cyberbullying is the use of electronic devices and information, such as e-mail, instant messaging (IM), text messages, mobile phones, pagers and web sites, to send or post cruel or harmful messages or images about an individual or a group. With nearly three-quarters of kids on line and many equipped with cell phones, the bully not only has the school yard, but the Internet highway to assault kids. And it's not just during recess; it's during school and at home.

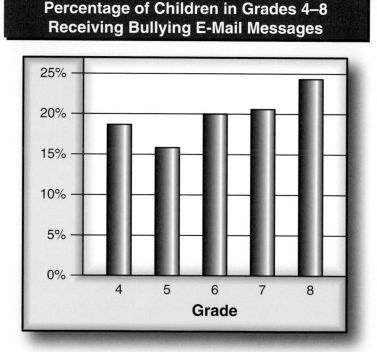

Percentage of Children in Grades 4–8 Receiving Bullying E-Mail Messages

Taken from: an i-SAFE America survey of students nationwide.

The law enforcement leaders of Fight Crime: Invest in Kids, a national, bipartisan, non-profit organization of more than 3,000 sheriffs, police chiefs, prosecutors, other law enforcement leaders and violence survivors, are investigating reports of cyberbullying in every community. But we wanted a national survey to know the full extent of cyberbullying. Fight Crime: Invest in Kids commissioned Opinion

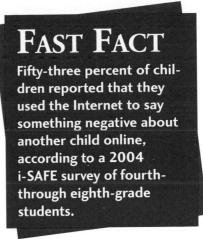

Research, a national, non-partisan polling firm to interview a national sample of 1,000 kids ages six to 17. The findings are disturbing. Millions of children are being cyberbullied and many of them are not telling anyone about it.

Kids Are Not Telling Anyone They're Being Cyberbullied

The results speak for themselves:

- One-third of all teens (ages 12 to 17) and one-sixth of children ages six to 11 said they have had mean, threatening or embarrassing things said about them online.
- 10 percent of the teens and four percent of the younger children said they were threatened with physical harm.
- The finding I find most scary—because of serious harm for kids—is that 16 percent of the teens and preteens who were victims of cyberbullying told no one about it. About half of children aged 6 to 11 told their parents about the hurtful messages. Only 30 percent of older kids told their parents.
- With a new school year about to begin, one out of six preteens and one out of 15 older kids are worried they will be bullied when they return to school.

Based on this research, Fight Crime: Invest in Kids estimates that more than 13 million children ages six to 17 are victims of cyberbullying. More than 2 million of those victims told no one about being attacked.

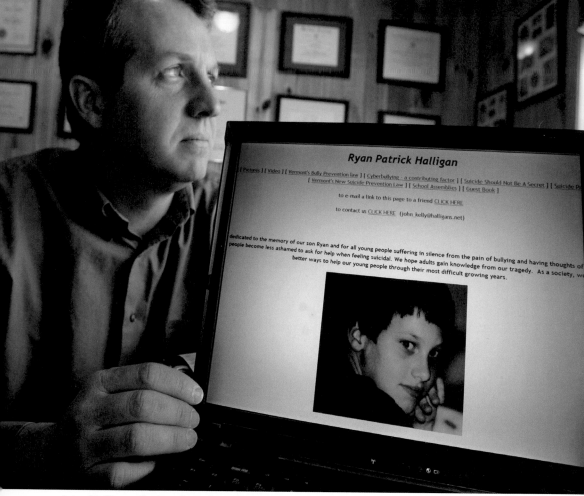

John Halligan displays the website devoted to his son, Ryan, who committed suicide as a result of being bullied online.

Bullies Today, Criminals Tomorrow

We need to take cyberbullying seriously for multiple reasons. First, in most states, cyberbullying is a crime. Second, what may not be a crime today, may be one tomorrow. We know that bullies in schools and playgrounds are more likely to grow up and commit crimes. From the recent survey, we now know that twice as many kids are victims of cyberbullying as they are of face-to-face bullying.

America's law enforcement leaders are providing families with 10 practical steps to delete cyberbullying from the current favorites list.

1. Kids should tell their parents, a teacher or the police if they have been cyberbullied or know other kids who have been cyberbullied.

2. Parents should insist that every school in America has a proven

anti-bullying program, such as the Olweus Bullying Prevention Program that addresses cyberbullying and other forms of bullying. The program can cut bullying in half.

3. Parents should insist that all schools establish a relationship with local law enforcement agencies so that they can help school officials deal with cyberbullying, including informing students that Internet and other electronic communication can be traced.

4. Parents should look for signs that their child might be a victim of cyberbullying, including having nightmares, avoiding school, acting sad or withdrawn, or suddenly showing disinterest in computers or rapidly switching screens.

5. Parents should discuss cyberbullying and bullying with their kids and what kinds of Internet activities the kids enjoy.

6. Parents should keep computers used by children in common areas of the home.

7. Emails, chats, text messages including instant messages and web pages sent or posted by bullies should be saved as evidence.

8. Parents should instruct their kids to not respond to bullying messages; if the messages continue, tell the sender to stop; block or filter all further messages; and if necessary, change their email address, account, username or phone number.

9. Kids should not give out ANY private information such as full names, addresses, phone numbers, personal identification numbers, passwords, school names or names of family members or friends. Kids should use a screen name different from their email address.

10. Families should file complaints with the Internet service provider, cell phone company or web site.

Anti-Bullying Laws Are Needed

Last, but not least, Congress should do its part to help every school have a bullying prevention program by passing the bullying prevention bill.

Cyberbullying is an insidious and invisible attack terrorizing many young people. It is a real and dangerous threat to the safety of America's kids, but one we can beat back by working together at home, school and in Congress.

EVALUATING THE AUTHOR'S ARGUMENTS:

In the viewpoint you just read, Larry Kopko mentions that more than 13 million children between the ages of six and seventeen have been victims of cyberbullying, and that more than 2 million of those children did not tell anyone. Why do you think some children do not tell their parents or another adult that they're being bullied?

Private Schools Can Fight Cyberbullying

Karla D. Shores

"Now they pull up Myspace.com, slam you in a blog, and click 'send.'"

In the following viewpoint, Karla D. Shores discusses how Catholic schools in South Florida are using the law to restrict what their students do on the Internet. Specifically, they are concerned about postings on Myspace.com that target their students. Public and private schools prevent children from accessing Web sites during the school day, but private Catholic schools in South Florida feel they need to discipline students who post abusive messages about and photos of classmates on the Internet from home. Karla D. Shores is a reporter for the *South Florida Sun-Sentinel*, in which this article appeared.

AS YOU READ, CONSIDER THE FOLLOWING QUESTIONS:

1. According to the author, why can't public schools restrict or monitor their students' use of the Internet at home while private schools can?
2. How many people use the Myspace.com Web site, according to the author?
3. In the article, how does Danielle Smith protect her privacy on the Myspace.com Web site?

Karla D. Shores, "South Florida Catholic Schools Seeks to Silence Cyberbullies," *South Florida Sun-Sentinel*, Jan. 29, 2006. Copyright © 2006 *South Florida Sun-Sentinel*. Reproduced by permission.

In the old days, school bullies stole your lunch money and passed mean notes about you in class.

Now they pull up Myspace.com, slam you in a blog, and click "send."

Public schools can do little more than strongly discourage students from posting derogatory language about fellow students because the writing happens away from the classroom. Most schools, private and public, install blocks that prevent students from accessing Web sites during school hours.

But private schools aren't bound by First Amendment rights when it comes to tawdry behavior online.

Punishing Kids for Cyberbullying from Home

As a step toward encouraging morality, combating school bullying and promoting Internet safety, South Florida Catholic schools are crafting policies to make culprits pay for their actions at home.

"There are borderline pornographic references about kids and statements that would not make someone feel comfortable coming to

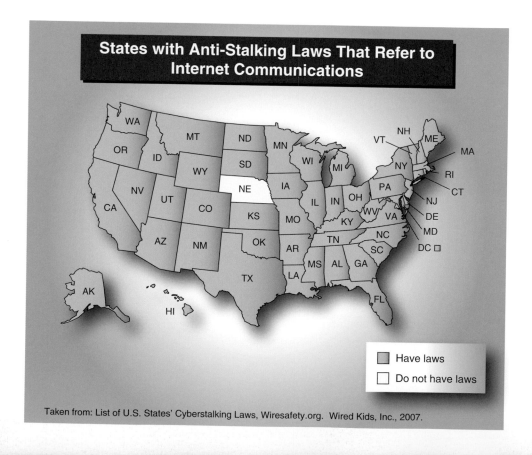

States with Anti-Stalking Laws That Refer to Internet Communications

Have laws

Do not have laws

Taken from: List of U.S. States' Cyberstalking Laws, Wiresafety.org. Wired Kids, Inc., 2007.

school," said Archdiocese of Miami Superintendent of Elementary Schools Kristen Hughes. "What's part of what used to be parent work has become principal work."

The Archdiocese of Miami, which includes Broward County, has fielded so many calls from Catholic schools over the past month, they're considering creating a penalty for degrading classmates online.

And the Diocese of Palm Beach County is working with attorneys to draft a policy against abusive postings on Web sites like Myspace. Neither organization has disclosed how it would penalize students for online misbehavior.

Myspace.com is a free, 2-year-old networking site [myspace.com was founded in 2003] young bloggers have elevated into an online diary phenomenon. For the younger set—many who first find Myspace while in middle school—it's second in importance to cell phones; they blog, post pictures of themselves and their friends, and many offer personal information, including where they attend school.

Attempts for a comment from Myspace were not successful.

The Web site has attracted more than 17 million users, according to www.wiredsafety.org, a nonprofit group specializing in online safety.

Myspace Is Not Safe for Children

Myspace is intended for bloggers ages 14 and older and invites users to report underage log-ons, but some parents say enforcement is lax. Additionally, there are no guarantees that people are who they purport to be.

For example, a 16-year-old Pompano Beach girl who says she attends Cardinal Gibbons in Fort Lauderdale lists 100 Myspace friends on her Web page. Among several photos of herself and friends is a prominent picture of one holding up a poster board that reads "I realy [sic] love Older Men!"

Legal experts say private schools and the dioceses are well within their rights to restrict or monitor the at-home use of the Internet. Public schools, because they are

> **FAST FACT**
>
> As of March 2007, forty-one states have antistalking statutes that specifically address cyberbullying (as "electronic communications").

Some schools believe that they can curb cyberbullying by restricting access to Web sites during school hours but others are looking for ways to discipline students who post violent or threatening messages even after hours.

government run, have no authority to restrict speech exercised by a student at home, said Randall Marshall, legal director of the American Civil Liberties Union of Florida.

Catholic schools are targeting Myspace because students complain to administrators about how they're being portrayed on the Web site.

Internet Safety Programs Help

Private school administrators in Palm Beach County, along with law enforcement officials, have organized Internet safety workshops for parents, said Diocese of Palm Beach County spokeswoman Alexis Walkenstein.

Some schools are already taking action. More than 100 parents whose children attend St. Mark Catholic School in Boynton Beach attended an Internet safety program at the school this month, said principal Marcia Seamans.

"We have a lot of parents who think their child is safe and this is a good thing, but actually they're safe at home but writing on the Internet to who knows where," said Seamans, adding that she will discipline students who use Myspace.com to abuse classmates.

Principal Paul Ott of Cardinal Gibbons High School said he began targeting use of the Web site after several students complained to him that they were being misrepresented on it. In a January school newsletter, the dean of discipline, Thomas Mahon, wrote, "[Cardinal Gibbons] and the Archdiocese will be making policy concerning 'My Space.Com' and the filth being published by some individuals."

"Young people being who they are, can be very hurtful," said Ott, who declined to explain the nature of the complaints. "You can sign on as somebody else and create whatever you want."

Danielle Smith, 15, a freshman at Pope John Paul II High School in Boca Raton, said she has a different view of Myspace because she uses it the "right" way.

"You just have to have a good head on your shoulders and not do something you'll regret later," she said. "Know what your parents would want you to do. And don't say you'll meet someone that you've never met before."

Smith said she uses only her school's initials on her Web site and uses a fake city and state. She said her Web page is private, which means only those she invites to her site can see her pictures and write to her.

Parents Need to Become Aware

Wendy Mitchler, whose two teens attend Cardinal Gibbons and St. Marks Episcopal School in Oakland Park, said a lot of headache at schools could be avoided if parents became more Myspace savvy.

"If they're locking you out of the room and every time you come to the computer they hit the 'escape' button, you know they can't be up to any good," Mitchler said.

Mitchler's 16-year-old son uses Myspace, but she forbade her 13-year-old daughter from creating her own Web site.

Mitchler said she would support administrators enforcing a "mild" policy against abusive behavior on Myspace. For example, detention would be OK, but it would be going to far to pull someone off the basketball team or the National Honor Society for slamming a classmate.

A Pope John Paul II High School parent, Diane Ferrazoli, said she made her 15-year-old daughter delete her Myspace Web site after she learned more about the site at an Internet safety program at her younger daughter's St. Mark Catholic School.

"Too bad public schools can't do it too and it couldn't just be a state thing because it's just too easy," Ferrazoli said. "Parents think they know but they really don't know what's going on."

EVALUATING THE AUTHOR'S ARGUMENTS:

In the viewpoint you just read, Karla D. Shores discusses how Catholic schools in South Florida are working to implement a plan that will punish students who post negative and nasty messages about other students on the Internet, even if they write these postings at home. Do you feel that any school, public or private, has the right to punish what a student does at home? Why or why not?

Chapter 3

How Can Bullying Be Reduced?

Some people believe that legislation can provide a means to reducing bullying.

Victims Should Fight Back Against Bullies

Pat Morgan

"What we have to do . . . is get rid of victims."

In the following viewpoint, Pat Morgan interviews Izzy Kalman about his views on bully prevention. Kalman, a psychologist and the author of *Bullies to Buddies*, lectures about using common sense to fight back against bullies by refusing to act like a victim. He contends that bullying is inevitable in our society and that it flourishes because schools and parents try to change the bully's behavior when it is the victim's behavior that needs to change. Kalman maintains that victims of bullying need to stop acting like victims and refuse to be bullied by ignoring the nasty taunts and comments they hear. Pat Morgan wrote this article for the *Palm Beach Post*.

AS YOU READ, CONSIDER THE FOLLOWING QUESTIONS:

1. According to the author, why does Izzy Kalman feel that bullying is protected under the Constitution?
2. What did the research cited by Kalman report about anti-bullying policies?
3. What advice did the author receive from his mother about teasing?

eople have a knee-jerk reaction when they hear that," said Kalman over lunch last month, while he was in West Palm Beach leading a seminar for school counselors and other mental health professionals. "They say I'm blaming the victims. I'm not blaming the victims, but I am saying that they are the ones who have the problem. Bullies don't have the problem. They aren't the ones committing suicide and shooting up schools. Those are the victims, and those are the ones whose behavior we need to change."

Kalman, who spent 26 years as a school psychologist and private psychotherapist, wants to make something clear. He is not saying bullying is good. He's saying it's inevitable, a natural byproduct of human nature. He's also saying that, to the extent it helps teach kids resilience and self-sufficiency, it's useful. And he's saying that, unless it causes physical harm, it's also legal, protected under the Constitution.

A student at DuPont Elementary School in Delaware plays the part of a victim during a skit demonstrating anti-bullying techniques.

"Our Constitution guarantees the right to free speech," he says. "And that means the right to tell someone they are a big, fat idiot if we want to. Kids today are growing up with the idea that nobody can ever say anything mean to them. We are raising a generation of emotional marshmallows. We're promoting learned helplessness. And I am really concerned that when these kids grow up, they are going to be unable to handle adversity of any kind, because we learn to handle adversity from dealing with the fairly simple difficulties of childhood."

Like being called a big, fat idiot by the class bully.

It's all about power.

It has been seven years since Eric Harris and Dylan Klebold went on a shooting rampage on April 20, 1999, at Columbine High School near Denver. The two teenagers, reportedly longtime targets for bullies, killed 12 students and a teacher and wounded 24 others before committing suicide.

Bullying hasn't stopped with the anti-bullying policies enacted by many schools after Columbine, says Kalman. And it never will stop, he says, until the victims—one by one—stop it. Guns won't do it, says Kalman. And neither will a zero-tolerance policy.

Kalman points to the work of Canadian psychologist David Smith, whose research (published in the December 2004 issue of *School Psychology Review*) found that 57 percent of anti-bullying policies had no measurable benefit, 14 percent yielded mild improvement and 29 percent actually made the problem worse.

"You can't teach tolerance with a zero-tolerance policy," Kalman says. "It's no big deal to be tolerant of people who are nice to you. The challenge is to tolerate people who aren't so nice. On top of that, 'zero tolerance for aggression' is a logical absurdity, because it ultimately requires that we use aggression to stop it."

FAST FACT

The First Amendment of the U.S. Constitution reads, "Congress shall make no law respecting an establishment of religion, or prohibiting the free exercise thereof; or abridging the freedom of speech, or of the press; or of the right of the people peaceably to assemble; and to petition the government for redress of grievances."

The way to end bullying is really, simple, says Kalman. Remove its power.

"The truth is, we all want power. That's human nature. But many of us don't want to admit it," Kalman says. "We go after the bullies because they are open about it. When you can get someone to make a fool of himself—yelling and getting all red-faced and maybe even crying—simply by calling him a name over and over again, that's power.

"And in honesty, it's also fun. It's entertaining to watch other people make fools of themselves. That's why we watch those home-video shows and those reality shows on TV. What do we laugh hardest at? People falling off things, losing control or making a complete idiot

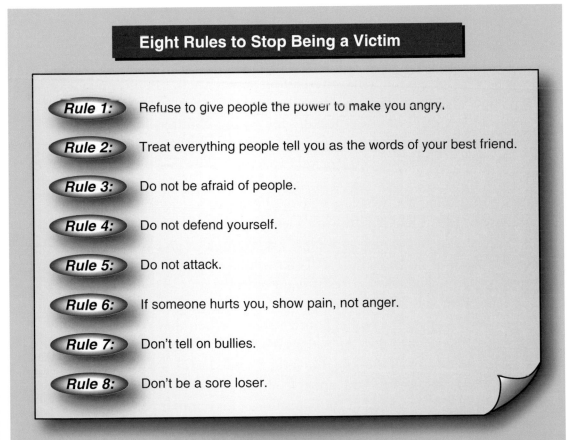

Eight Rules to Stop Being a Victim

Rule 1: Refuse to give people the power to make you angry.

Rule 2: Treat everything people tell you as the words of your best friend.

Rule 3: Do not be afraid of people.

Rule 4: Do not defend yourself.

Rule 5: Do not attack.

Rule 6: If someone hurts you, show pain, not anger.

Rule 7: Don't tell on bullies.

Rule 8: Don't be a sore loser.

Taken from: Izzy Kalman, "Stop Thinking Like a Victim! Applying Eight Rules Will Make You a Winner," *Personal Excellence*, June 2006. Copyright © 2006 Leadership Excellence. Reproduced by permission.

of themselves in some way. They could be seriously hurt, and we're laughing our heads off."

Even Identifying a true bully can be difficult, he says, because a child may act like a bully in one setting and a victim in another. It all depends on the balance of power.

"Who among us can guarantee that their own child will never be mean?" Kalman asks.

Once again, mother knows best

Kalman's seminars—as well as his book, CD and Web site—are filled with sample scenarios in which he often has seminar participants play the bully to his victim (a practice he highly recommends for educators, counselors and parent, pointing out how much kids love it when adults are willing to look foolish). His delivery is as much stand-up comedian as it is psychology professional. And his tenets, he freely admits, are hardly original—or even modern. They are based on ancient wisdom revealed to us by Mother Nature, our Founding Fathers and various philosophers throughout the ages.

Like my mother. And probably yours.

As I sat through Kalman's entertaining presentation, I found myself agreeing with his premise while still questioning the effectiveness of some of his suggestions, especially for young children whose self-confidence may be shaky. It's pretty hard for most adults I know to ignore rude or mean behavior, and expecting a 7-year-old to be able to "not care" when someone is saying horrible things to her—or more likely, excluding her, which is a favored bullying tactic of girls—is a tall order. Still, I had to admit it's a lesson worth trying to teach.

Kalman's answer to such concerns: "I don't think we give kids enough credit. You'd be surprised how well even young kids understand this. If they are being bullied, they really want to find a way to make it stop, and they probably know from experience that fighting back or getting angry or telling on the bullies hasn't worked. When they try this and it works, they are thrilled. After that, it's easy for them."

I also found myself thinking the room should be filled with parents rather than educators and therapists (Kalman does sometimes speak to parent groups). As several of the educators at his seminar pointed out, schools literally cannot afford to ignore bullying, even in its milder forms, for fear of being held legally liable if a child is harmed on the school premises. But if parents can help their kids learn to ignore

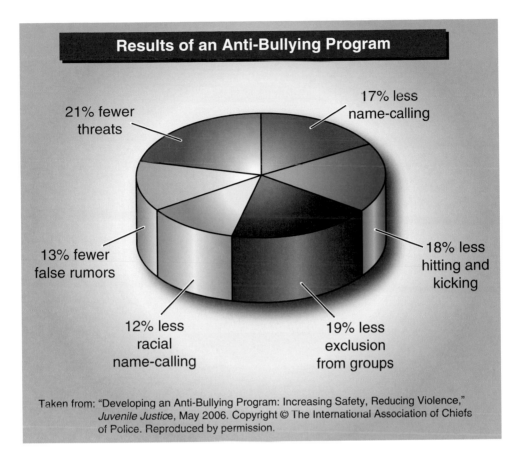

Results of an Anti-Bullying Program

21% fewer threats

17% less name-calling

13% fewer false rumors

18% less hitting and kicking

12% less racial name-calling

19% less exclusion from groups

Taken from: "Developing an Anti-Bullying Program: Increasing Safety, Reducing Violence," *Juvenile Justice*, May 2006. Copyright © The International Association of Chiefs of Police. Reproduced by permission.

certain types of bullying, it may prevent it from escalating or becoming chronic.

But mostly, I found myself repeatedly recalling the advice my mother always offered when I'd complain about being mercilessly teased by any of my eight older siblings.

"He only teases you because you get upset," she'd say patiently, time after time. "Stop getting upset, and he'll stop teasing you."

That's as succinct a description of Kalman's techniques as I could ever think up.

My mother never finished high school. But, as the highly educated Kalman rather gleefully notes, his method is not the product of psychological theory, scientific research or academic rumination.

It is, quite simply, "about experience and common sense." Both of which my mom has in spades.

It's a funny thing about parents: The longer you live, the smarter they get.

EVALUATING THE AUTHOR'S ARGUMENTS:

In the viewpoint you just read, Izzy Kalman maintains that bullying is protected under our Constitution because of the right to free speech, even if we do not agree with what's being said. Do you agree with this? Does someone have the right to say something that's mean and hurtful to someone else? Should this be protected as the right to free speech? In this post-Columbine, zero-tolerance world, Izzy Kalman is something of a revolutionary. He agrees that bullying is a big problem. But he contends that getting rid of bullies is not the solution (and, in fact, is not even possible). What we have to do, he says, is get rid of victims.

The Community Must Help Victims Fight Back Against Bullies

"The key components of the bullying intervention program . . . are increased adult supervision in all areas of the school, increased consequences for bullying behavior, and a clear message that bullying will not be tolerated."

Linda Starr

In the following viewpoint, Linda Starr writes about the Olweus Bullying Prevention Program, which was developed by psychologist Dan Olweus after three Norwegian students killed themselves after having been badly bullied. The program, which has since been implemented in many schools around the world, involves adults, schools, and students in taking proactive and positive steps to reduce bullying. It emphasizes that schools are obligated to protect their students from bullying and to provide a positive learning environment. Linda Starr wrote this article for *Education World*.

AS YOU READ, CONSIDER THE FOLLOWING QUESTIONS:
1. According to the author, what were the results of the Bullying Prevention Program developed by Dan Olweus in Norway two years after it had been put into place?
2. What actions should school bullies take because of their bullying, according to the Olweus Bullying Prevention Program?
3. According to the Olweus Bullying Prevention Program, at what point in school is the problem of bullying generally at its worst?

In 1982, three Norwegian boys, ages 10 through 14, committed suicide, apparently as a result of severe bullying by their classmates. The event triggered shock and outrage, led to a national campaign against bullying behavior, and finally, resulted in the development of a systematic school-based bullying intervention program. That program, developed by psychologist Dan Olweus, was tested with more than 2,500 students in Bergen, Norway. Within two years, incidents of school bullying had dropped by more than 50 percent. Since then, a number of countries, including England, Germany, and the United States, have implemented Olweus's program with similar results.

FAST FACT

According to www.bully beware.com, 71 percent of teachers believe they intervene in bullying situations, while only 25 percent of students report that the teachers do.

Changing a Bully's Behavior

Olweus based the program on principles derived from research into behavior modification techniques for aggressive or violent children. The program restructures the learning environment to create a social climate characterized by supportive adult involvement, positive adult role models, firm limits, and consistent, noncorporal sanctions for bullying behavior.

In order to effectively accomplish its goals of reducing existing bullying problems and preventing the development of future problems, the program leads teachers, administrators, and staff through a series of tasks that make them aware of the extent of the bullying problem and help them solve it. Those tasks include the following:

What Schools Can Do

- a bullying survey to determine the extent of the problem.
- a conference day to educate teachers, administrators, school staff, parents, students, and community members about bullying behaviors, response strategies, and available resources.
- increased supervision in the cafeteria, hallways, bathrooms, and on the playground, where most bullying behavior occurs.
- a coordinating group—typically consisting of an administrator; a teacher from each grade level; a guidance counselor, psychologist, and/or school nurse; and parent and student representatives—to manage the program and evaluate its success.
- ongoing meetings between parents and school staff.
- discussions of bullying issues at regularly scheduled PTO meetings.

Dennis Embry, a child psychologist, created the Peace Builders program that has successfully curbed bullying in schools.

Make Changes in the Classroom

- a curriculum that promotes kindness, communication, cooperation, and friendship and includes lessons and activities stressing empathy, anger management, and conflict resolution skills.

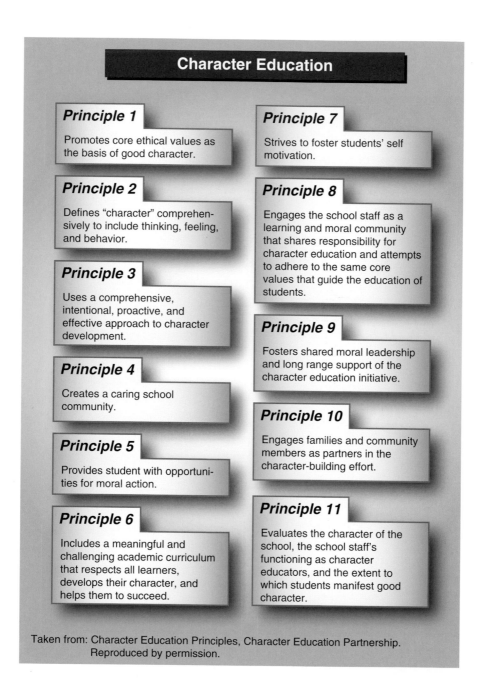

Character Education

Principle 1
Promotes core ethical values as the basis of good character.

Principle 2
Defines "character" comprehensively to include thinking, feeling, and behavior.

Principle 3
Uses a comprehensive, intentional, proactive, and effective approach to character development.

Principle 4
Creates a caring school community.

Principle 5
Provides student with opportunities for moral action.

Principle 6
Includes a meaningful and challenging academic curriculum that respects all learners, develops their character, and helps them to succeed.

Principle 7
Strives to foster students' self motivation.

Principle 8
Engages the school staff as a learning and moral community that shares responsibility for character education and attempts to adhere to the same core values that guide the education of students.

Principle 9
Fosters shared moral leadership and long range support of the character education initiative.

Principle 10
Engages families and community members as partners in the character-building effort.

Principle 11
Evaluates the character of the school, the school staff's functioning as character educators, and the extent to which students manifest good character.

Taken from: Character Education Principles, Character Education Partnership. Reproduced by permission.

- class rules against bullying. Rules should be brief and clear. Olweus suggests the following examples:
    1. We will not bully other students.
    2. We will try to help students who are bullied.
    3. We will include students who might be left out.
- immediate consequences for aggressive behavior and immediate rewards for inclusive behavior. Possible sanctions include having the bully
    1. apologize;
    2. discuss the incident with the teacher, principal, and/or parents;
    3. pay for damaged belongings;
    4. spend time in the office or another classroom;
    5. forfeit recess or other privileges.
- weekly meetings to communicate to students clear and consistently enforced expectations and to engage them as resources in preventing bullying behavior.
- ongoing communication with parents.

One Person Can Make a Difference
- serious talks with bullies and victims.
- serious talks with the parents of bullies and victims.
- role playing of non-aggressive behavior with bullies.
- role playing of assertive behavior with victims.

The key components of the bullying intervention program, according to Olweus, are increased adult supervision in all areas of the school, increased consequences for bullying behavior, and a clear message that bullying will not be tolerated.

Adults Must Take Responsibility
Olweus also recommends that for a bullying intervention program to be successful, schools must do the following:
- Place primary responsibility for solving the problem with the adults at school rather than with parents or students.
- Project a clear moral stand against bullying.
- Include both systems-oriented and individual-oriented components.
- Set long-term and short-term goals.

- Target the entire school population, not just a few problem students.
- Make the program a permanent component of the school environment, not a temporary remedial program.
- Implement strategies that have a positive effect on students and on the school climate that go beyond the problem of bullying.

Change Behavior at an Early Age

Bullying behavior, according to Dr. Olweus, is evident even in preschool and the problem peaks in middle school. It's important, therefore, that bullying intervention strategies be implemented as early as possible. Even if only a small number of students are directly involved, Olweus points out, every student who witnesses bullying is affected in some way. Even students who initially sympathize with or defend victims may eventually come to view bullying as acceptable if responsible adults fail to say otherwise. Over time, ignoring—or being ignorant of—bullying behavior will result in a social climate that fosters bullying, fighting, truancy, and other social and learning problems in all students.

"The school," said Olweus, "has a responsibility to stop bullying behavior and create a safe learning environment for all students."

EVALUATING THE AUTHOR'S ARGUMENTS:

In this viewpoint, Linda Starr discusses the Olweus Bullying Prevention Program, which places responsibility for solving school bullying with adults. In the previous viewpoint, Izzy Kalman argues that the victims should be responsible for solving this problem. Which argument do you feel is more persuasive? Why?

Viewpoint 3

Regulating Recess Will Help Prevent Bullying

Sandy Louey

"Concerned about safety and injuries and worried about bullying, violence, self-esteem and lawsuits, school officials have clamped down on the traditional games from years past."

In the following viewpoint, Sandy Louey discusses the trends toward limiting what children are allowed to play during recess. Games such as dodgeball have been banned; and, in certain schools, children cannot play tag because someone might be pushed or grabbed. There is an emphasis on having the kids playing organized games, such as relay races. Opponents of this trend contend that children need the chance and freedom to play whatever they'd like to play to learn to be creative and also learn to compete with one another. This article was published in the *Sacramento Bee*.

AS YOU READ, CONSIDER THE FOLLOWING QUESTIONS:
1. According to the author, why aren't children allowed to push one another on the swing at recess?
2. According to a school principal in the article, what three things must schools try to teach kids?

Sandy Louey, "Recess Gets Regulated: Worried About Safety, Schools Restrict Traditional Games," *Sacramento Bee*, August 22, 2004. Reproduced by permission.

During recess at Woodridge Elementary School, a girl walked up to the foursquare court, wanting to join the game.

"You want to play," Briauna Ford, a sixth-grader, told her. "You got to read the rules."

Eight rules for Switched, a game Briauna and her friends made up, were scrawled on a piece of notebook paper: Rule No. 2: "You must say 'switch, switch' two times to begin the game." Rule No. 6: "Make right choices no yelling."

Briauna and her friends drew up the regulations so the game wouldn't end up in shouting matches and hurt feelings—which could get Switched tossed off the playground in the Rio Linda Union School District.

Recess may be child's play, but it's serious business to adults. Dodgeball has spawned a hit summer movie and a TV game show. But as school doors begin to open again around the Sacramento region, kids thumping each other with a large inflated rubber ball isn't something you are likely to see on school playgrounds.

Safety Comes First

Concerned about safety and injuries and worried about bullying, violence, self-esteem and lawsuits, school officials have clamped down on the traditional games from years past.

Gone from many blacktops are tag, dodgeball and any game involving bodily contact. In are organized relay races and adult-supervised activities.

"It's fun stuff," said Azia Orum, a Rio Linda sixth-grader. "We just can't do it. People get hurt."

Kids Need a Chance to Run Around

The restrictions trouble some early-childhood experts and parents. Recess is usually the only part of the school day where kids can do what they want. Experts say free play helps kids learn how to cooperate, socialize and work out conflicts.

"We ask kids to work hard," said Roberta Raymond, principal at

Woodridge. "They need frequent breaks to give their minds a rest."

What games students can—or can't—play at recess varies. Each school tailors the rules to its own needs.

Growing enrollments in some districts make firm rules all the more important, educators say, though kids at lunch or recess are always difficult to monitor.

Maeola Beitzel Elementary School in the Elk Grove Unified School District has about 1,200 students, while Natomas Park Elementary School in the

Natomas Unified School District has about 1,100 students. Both are year-round schools, with at least 800 enrolled at any one time.

At Natomas Park, that means three recesses in the morning and two in the afternoon, along with five lunches for grades one to five. Up to six yard-duty supervisors roam during lunch.

Kids Aren't Allowed to Push Each Other

Games where kids chase each other—tag or even cops and robbers—are generally banned in Natomas Unified's elementary schools. No grabbing or pushing is allowed.

At Natomas Park, students can only toss and catch a football—tackling or blocking isn't permitted. But the no-contact rule applies beyond the grade-school gridiron.

During lunch recess one recent afternoon, yard supervisor Janice Hudson spotted a first-grader pushing a girl on the swing.

"Do not push," Hudson told the student. "Let her push herself, please."

"One person can be a little stronger than the other," she said as she walked away.

During second-grade lunch, Hudson set up relay races so students could run within the rules. The whistle blew and the racers took off, dashing down the five lanes. A crowd screamed "Go! Go!" Each of the more than 30 students got a chance to run.

Many schools have defined specific policies banning games or activities that could lead to injuries or ostracism.

Safety, Bullying, and Lawsuits Are Concerns

Natomas Park administrators say physical safety was the main reason they instituted restrictions. But they admit to worrying about bullying and potential lawsuits from parents.

At Maeola Beitzel Elementary, Janis Mayse, the mother of a fifth-grader, doesn't think the fun is worth it if a game is played to the detriment of another child.

"All of us want to hang on to the games we played as kids," she said, "but we have to keep an open mind that there are games that kids can get a benefit from without hurting one another."

An Emphasis on Teaching Character

Many see the recess restrictions as part of larger cultural shifts. Schools now must craft lesson plans on responsibility, honesty and violence prevention, Maeola Beitzel Principal Judy Hunt-Brown said. And those lessons, among other things, fit neatly into the structured, organized play so prevalent on today's schoolyard.

"To some degree, the school has needed to take a larger role in teaching children how to play with each other—the whole taking turns, how to deal with conflict," Hunt-Brown said.

Tightened restrictions on playgrounds are part of the growing trend to more strictly control what happens during the school day. Child behavior experts are concerned that strict rules for play threaten to straitjacket students' creativity.

Children Need Free Play

Recess is supposed to be spontaneous play. The unstructured time helps fuel the imagination, said Dolores Stegelin, associate professor of early childhood education at Clemson University.

"It encourages creativity. It strengthens social development when they can be creative and plan something together and set up their own rules. It allows for leadership," said Stegelin, a member of the Association for the Study of Play. "Adults need to be there, but there needs to be more time for kids to be innovative and do their own activity."

Dodgeball Teaches Kids About Life

Dodgeball teaches students eye-hand coordination and gross motor skills. Getting singled out and eliminated from competition is part of life, said Tom Reed, professor of early childhood education at the University of South Carolina Upstate in Spartanburg.

"Life is not always fair," said Reed, also a member of the Association for the Study of Play. "You don't get what you want. Things like this are learned on the playground."

That's what worries Kellie Randle. A former teacher and a parent of a student at Joseph Sims Elementary School in Elk Grove, Randle believes kids aren't as creative as they once were.

"I'm concerned about the direction of a society where kids are encouraged not to run and play," she said. "If you take away running, freeze tag and red light, green light, you're taking away a big part of childhood."

At Woodridge, the bell signaling the end of summer school recess rang. The Switched players got ready to return to class.

Rule No. 5: If two people get a corner, choose a number between one and 20. The person who is closest gets the corner.

Rule No. 8: If you make bad choices, you must leave the game.

"It went better today with the rules," said 11-year-old Erma Murphy. Her friends nodded in agreement.

EVALUATING THE AUTHOR'S ARGUMENTS:

In the viewpoint you just read, Sandy Louey writes about the move toward restricting what children can play during recess. In some school districts, students are allowed to play only relay races and other adult-supervised games. Opponents believe that not allowing children to decide for themselves what they want to play outweighs the chance of bullying or injury. Do you agree with the opponents' view? Why or why not?

Regulating Recess Will Not Help Prevent Bullying

Steven Rushin

"[O]ne school cancelled recess for eighth-graders in an effort to end bullying, which is a little like scalping in an effort to end dandruff."

In the following viewpoint, *Sports Illustrated* columnist Steve Rushin argues against the move to ban recess for many students in an attempt to reduce bullying and injury. He maintains that children playing without adult supervision will learn how to better deal with life as adults, and the need for a chance to play is more important than the possibility of bullying or injury. Children's games, such as Duck, Duck, Goose, and Mother, May I, have taken on a new— and, in Rushin's opinion, an unfair one— connotation in which they are no longer simply games that children play but are acts of aggression and violence.

AS YOU READ, CONSIDER THE FOLLOWING QUESTIONS:

1. According to Rushin, what percentage of first- and second-graders do not get recess? Sixth-graders?
2. What are the primary reasons that recess is being banned in some schools, in the opinion of the author?
3. What types of playground equipment will you not see on playgrounds anymore, according to the author?

Steven Rushin, "Give the Kids a Break," *Sports Illustrated*, Dec. 4, 2006. Reproduced by permission.

Four square and seven years ago we had recess: 20 minutes, twice a day, of Darwinian contests whose very names—king of the hill, capture the flag, keep-away, dodgeball—screamed survival of the fittest. After all, monkey in the middle isn't just a playground game; it describes the chain of human evolution.

Most of these games were passed down like heirlooms. They crossed continents and centuries with only small modifications, surviving into the modern age with names such as duck, duck, goose; Mother, may I; and Miss Mary Mack. Ancient Greeks jumped rope, Caesar's subjects played a form of jacks, and blindman's bluff was played in the court of Henry VIII. Pity, then, that none of these games may survive the decade, and for one deeply depressing reason: Red rover, red rover, recess is over.

Or it is for many children. According to the National PTA, nearly 40% of U.S. elementary schools "have either eliminated or are considering eliminating recess." Twenty to 30 percent of schools offer 15 or fewer minutes of daily recess. Lifers at Leavenworth get more time

Some people believe that children benefit from the chance to compete with each other without direct adult supervision.

in the exercise yard. And the U.S. Department of Education reports that 7% of all U.S. first- and second-graders—and 13% of all sixth-graders—get no recess whatsoever.

How ever did this happen to the fabled fourth R? For starters, increased preparation for standardized tests mandated by No Child Left Behind leaves little time for recess. That legislation was passed by Congress, which through Sunday had spent 138 days in recess during this session,

FAST FACT

According to a PTA survey, more than 70 percent of teachers and parents surveyed believe that recess helps children with their social development, and more than 50 percent of PTA leaders agree that children are less disruptive in class if they've had recess.

safe in the knowledge that eight-year-olds can't vote. In fairness to school administrators, no one should have to choose between childhood ignorance and childhood obesity. But there are lots of other reasons for the recess recession.

One is fear of injury. Willett Elementary School in Attleboro, Mass., has been roundly ridiculed for banning tag and other so-called chase games. But similar bans were imposed long ago by many other schools in places such as Spokane; Cheyenne, Wyo.; and Suburban Charleston, S.C. Attleboro merely fell in line behind them. Trouble is, life is a chase game. At my elementary school every recess ended like Round 8 of a prizefight: with a bell, the mending of cuts and at least two parties forced to sit in a corner.

That kind of unsupervised play literally left its mark on me. The scar on my forehead? I hit a pipe while playing tag in the basement. My left front tooth? Knocked out by a thrown baseball as I daydreamed in the park. And those were just the accidents, independent of the teenage Torquemadas who intentionally inflicted all manner of torture. There were no junior high Geneva Conventions, and so almost everyone endured noogies, wedgies, swirlies, snuggies, sudsies, melvins, wet willies, pink bellies, Indian burns, Russian haircuts and Hertz doughnuts—and a litany of other poetic means of coercion.

That was then, this is now. Last year a 15-year-old boy in Gold Hill, Ore., was charged with offensive physical touching for giving a

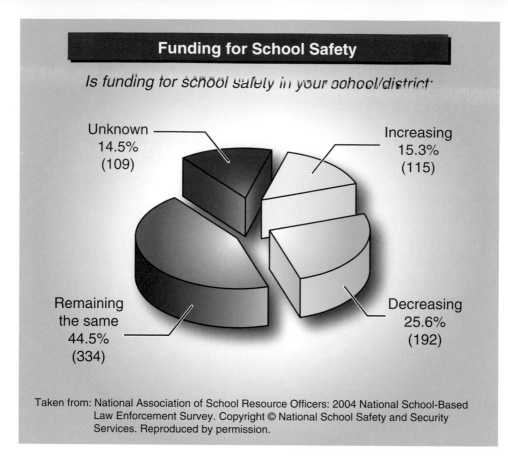

Funding for School Safety

Is funding for school safety in your school/district:

Unknown
14.5%
(109)

Increasing
15.3%
(115)

Remaining
the same
44.5%
(334)

Decreasing
25.6%
(192)

Taken from: National Association of School Resource Officers: 2004 National School-Based Law Enforcement Survey. Copyright © National School Safety and Security Services. Reproduced by permission.

13-year-old boy a purple nurple. And therein lie two other reasons that recess is receding: 1) playground bullies and 2) fear of lawsuits over injuries incurred on school grounds. In Maine one school canceled recess for eighth-graders in an effort to end bullying, which is a little like scalping in an effort to end dandruff.

It's a jungle out there, but you'll be hard pressed on most playgrounds to find a jungle gym, or monkey bars, or stainless-steel slides that in the summer months sizzle like a fajita skillet. Many seesaws are built with springs instead of the fulcrums that allowed one kid to jump off at the bottom, causing the other to drop abruptly, as if down an elevator shaft. And every piece of bubble-wrapped playground equipment—excuse me, playscape equipment—is festooned with labels that warn of deadly consequences for the smallest Misuse.

If all of this has you saying, "Give me a break," you've just voiced a universal human need. We all need a break. Some Teamsters get two 15-minute breaks per shift, the Supreme Court is in recess from July to October, and the third Thursday of every June is National Recess at Work Day, whose founder, Rich DiGirolamo, suggests that adults drop whatever they're doing next June 21 [2007] and "play tag and dodgeball, jump rope and eat watermelon."

Surely seven-year-olds deserve to do the same. And so National Recess Week was observed in September [2006], with Recess Rallies in schools around America. The PTA and the Cartoon Network are sponsoring a Rescuing Recess campaign. Something called the American Association for the Child's Right to Play is also eager to resuscitate recess.

All of them agree with G.K. Chesterton, who wrote, "Earth is a task garden; heaven is a playground."

EVALUATING THE AUTHOR'S ARGUMENTS:

In the viewpoint you just read, Steve Rushin writes that "life is a chase game." Do you agree that playing games at recess helps to prepare you for life as an adult? Why or why not?

Bullying in America

- The National Education Association estimates that 160,000 children miss school every day because of their anxiety about being bullied or harassed.
- An article in a 2001 issue of the *Journal of the Medical Association* estimated that approximately 30 percent of students in grades six through ten are bullies, bullied, or both.
- There are four types of bullying: physical, verbal, nonverbal or emotional, and cyberbullying.

The 2000 Maine Project Against Bullying survey of third-graders in Maine found that:

- Forty-eight percent of children said the situation became better after they told someone they'd been bullied, 15.3 percent said it became worse, 21.7 percent said nothing changed, and 5.9 percent reported that they never told anyone.
- More boys reported being bullied more by another boy (30.1 percent) than by a group of boys (17.7 percent) while girls reported being bullied more by a boy (18.9 percent) than by another girl (13.2 percent).

According to the Families and Work Institute's 2004 Ask the Children: Youth and Violence Survey:

- Sixty-six percent of students had been gossiped about or teased at least once in the past month while 25 percent reported that they'd been gossiped or teased about five times or more.
- Fifty-seven percent gossiped about or teased other kids at least once, and 12 percent had done so five times or more in the past month.

According to a 2005 Harris Interactive Poll conducted for the Gay, Lesbian and Straight Education Network:

- Sixty-five percent of teenagers said that they had been either physically or verbally assaulted or harassed because of their gender, sexual orientation, gender expression, disability, religion, race-ethnicity, or their actual or perceived appearance.

- Thirty-nine percent of students were frequently harassed because of the way they look, and 33 percent were harassed because they are or were thought to be gay, lesbian, or bisexual.

According to the 2006 Indicators of School Crime and Safety from the National Center for Education Statistics:

- Thirty percent of white students ages twelve to eighteen, 28.5 percent of African American students, and 22.3 percent of Hispanic students reported being bullied during a six-month period.
- More girls (29.2 percent) than boys (27.1 percent) reported being bullied.
- A 2002 U.S. Secret Service report stated that 75 percent of school shootings can be connected to bullying.

Girls, Boys, and Bullying

A 2001 National Institute of Child Health and Human Development survey of students found that:

- Thirteen percent had bullied others but had not been bullied themselves, 11 percent were victims only, and 6 percent were both bullies and victims.
- Bullying takes place most often during grades six through eight.

According to a 2003 National Institute of Child Health and Human Development survey of students:

- Of boys who reported bullying others at least once a week, 52.2 percent carried a weapon in the past month, 43.1 percent brought a weapon to school, 45.7 percent had been hurt during a fight, and 38.7 percent fought frequently.
- Of boys who did not bully others, 13.4 percent carried a weapon in the past month, 7.9 percent brought a weapon to school, 16.2 percent had been hurt during a fight, and 8.3 percent fought frequently.

According to bullying expert Dan Olweus:

- Most children are victims of verbal bullying.
- Boys are more likely to be victims of physical bullying than girls, and girls are more likely to exclude others socially.

Effects of Having Been Bullied

Bullying Online's 2006 National Survey found that:

- Of adults who reported being bullied as children, 20 percent said they had lost their confidence, 13 percent reported that it affected their relationships, 9 percent reported that they had been suicidal, 8 percent said they had gotten treatment for mental health issues, and 7 percent said it affected their ability to get a job.
- Seventy-eight percent of adults reported having been bullied more than five times at school.

Cyberbullying

According to a 2005–2006 survey by i-SAFE's National Assessment Center:

- Twenty-two percent of students reported that they know another student who has been bullied online, 19 percent said that they used the Internet to say something cruel to someone else, and 12 percent reported having become distressed themselves by something an online stranger said to them.
- Fifty-eight percent of students say that they have used the Internet illegally, inappropriately, or unsafely.

Bullycide

- The term *bullycide* was coined by authors Neil Marr and Tim Field in their book *Bullycide: Death at Playtime*, which explores the stories of children who have committed suicide as a result of having been bullied.
- There were 517 suicides of young people between the ages of ten and twenty-four from 1998 to 2002.

Organizations to Contact

Bullycide in America

Web site: www.bullycide.org

Bullycide is the term used to describe a child who commits suicide as the result of bullying. The Bullycide in America Web site was created by Brenda High, the founder of BullyPolice.com, after her son, Jared, committed suicide after having been bullied in school for years. It contains the stories of children who committed suicide after having been bullied, as told by their mothers. Other material on the site includes information about speakers who can make presentations about bullycide.

Bullying Online

Windsor House, Cornwall Road
Harrogate HG1 2PW England
e-mail: help@bullying.co.uk
Web site: www.bullying.co.uk

Bullying Online is a charity that works with schools, youth groups, and the police to help reduce school bullying. The Web site includes information about dealing with bullies, cyberbullying, racist bullying, bullying in sports, and antibullying policies for students, parents, and schools.

Bully Police USA, Inc.

(509) 547-1052
Web site: www.bullypolice.org

Established by Brenda High, Bully Police USA is an advocacy group devoted to helping bullied children and to passing antibullying laws in every state. Information on the Web site includes updated information about the status of antibullying legislation in each state, recommended antibullying programs and speakers, links to antibullying groups in each state, and suggestions for parents to help their bullied child.

BullyStoppers.com

72 Molly Pitcher Lane
Freehold, NJ 07728
(732) 547-2603
e-mail: bullystoppers@yahoo.com
Web site: www.bullystoppers.com

BullyStoppers.com was created by Tom Letson, the student assistance counselor and program coordinator for the Howell Township School District in New Jersey. The goal of the Web site is to encourage kids to report incidents of bullying in school and on school buses by allowing them to do so anonymously. Schools can then use the information to investigate the problem. Material on the site includes the bullying report form; tips and tools for students, parents, and schools; school threat assessment information; and links to bullying resources in each state.

Center for the Study and Prevention of Violence (CSPV)

Institute of Behavioral Science, University of Colorado at Boulder
1877 Broadway, Suite 601
Boulder, CO 80302
(303) 492-1032
e-mail: cspv@colorado.edu
Web site: www.colorado.edu/cspv/safeschools

The CSPV was founded in 1992 to provide information and assistance to organizations dedicated to preventing violence, particularly youth violence. The Safe Communities~Safe Schools program was created in 1999 to provide antibullying lessons, recommendations, and programs to schools. The site includes facts sheets, links to publications on school violence, and research.

i-SAFE, Inc.

5900 Pasteur Court, Suite 100
Carlsbad, CA 92008
(760) 603-7911
Web site: www.isafe.org

I-SAFE's goal is to educate children and teens about how to use the Internet safely. It offers interactive curriculum, which includes cyberbullying, cybersafety, personal security, and predator identification, to children in kindergarten through twelfth grade in each state. I-SAFE works with parents, community leaders, and law enforcement officials to promote appropriate Internet behavior and use. The Web site includes National Assessment Center surveys that provide current information about Internet attitudes and behaviors, as well as a student mentor program.

National Crime Prevention Council (NCPC)
1000 Connecticut Avenue, NW, Thirteenth Floor,
Washington, DC 20036
(202) 466-6272 • fax: (202) 296-1356
Web site: www.ncpc.org
The NCPC is a branch of the U.S. Department of Justice. Through its programs and education materials, the council works to teach Americans how to reduce crime and to address its causes, including bullying. It provides readers with information on bullying prevention and cyberbullying.

U.S. Health Resources and Services Administration's National Bullying Prevention Campaign
e-mail: comment@hrsa.gov
Web site: www.stopbullyingnow.hrsa.gov
The Stop Bullying Now! Web site is run by the U.S. Health Resources and Services Administration. It contains material for kids, including describing bullying, information about the effects of bullying, what to do about bullying, games, Webisodes, and online polls. There also is information about cyberbullying, resource material, and data for families and teachers.

WiredSafety.org
e-mail: askparry@wiredsafety.org
Web site: www.wiredsafety.org
Founded by Parry Aftab, WiredSafety.org's goal is to educate and protect children of all ages from cyberabuse, including cyberbullying, cyberstalking, hacking, sexual harassment, and identity theft. The Web site's features include cybercrime report forms; safe Web sites; information for parents, children, educators, and librarians; cybercrime law enforcement experts; and a tutorial on sexual predators.

For Further Reading

Books

Elizabeth A. Barton, *Bully Prevention: Tips and Strategies for School Leaders and Classroom Teachers*. Thousand Oaks, CA: Corwin Press, 2006. Offers role-playing examples for students and antibullying intervention strategies, and examines the interaction between bullies, the bullied, and bystanders.

Allan L. Beane and Linda Beane, *Bully Free Bulletin Boards, Posters and Banners: Creative Displays for a Safe and Caring School, Grades K-8*. Minneapolis, MN: Free Spirit Publishing, 2006. Provides materials to help schools implement antibullying programs.

Jose Bolton and Stan Graeve, *No Room for Bullies: From the Classroom to Cyberspace Teaching Respect, Stopping Abuse, and Rewarding Kindness*. Boys Town, NE: Boys Town Press, 2005. Discusses various forms of bullying, including cyberbullying, social exclusion, physical violence, and sexual abuse, and offers suggestions for creating a safe environment.

Barbara Coloroso, *The Bully, the Bullied, and the Bystander: From Pre-School to High School—How Parents and Teachers Can Help Break the Cycle of Violence*. New York: HarperCollins, 2004. The author examines how bullying is learned and how the bully, bullied, and bystander can learn to change their ways and offers advice about dealing with cliques, hazing, taunting, and sexual bullying.

Dewey G. Cornell, *School Violence: Fears Versus Facts*. Mahwah, NJ: Lawrence Erlbaum Associates, 2006. The author explores misconceptions about school bullying and violence and argues that certain programs used to combat school violence, such as school uniforms and zero-tolerance policies, are not as effective as school-based violence prevention policies and mental health services.

Stan Davis with Julia Davis, *Schools Where Everyone Belongs: Practical Strategies for Reducing Bullying*. Champaign, IL: Research Press, 2007. Describes methods for reducing bullying, which include establishing connections between students and teachers, creating effective discipline procedures, encouraging bystanders to take action, involving parents, and teaching kids to take responsibility for their behavior.

Merry L. Gumm, *Help! I'm in Middle School . . . How Will I Survive?* Douglass, KS: NSR Publications, 2004. The author—a teacher—offers middle-school students advice about dealing with issues facing kids, including bullies, harassment, and friends.

Izzy Kalman, *From Bullies to Buddies: How to Turn Your Enemies into Friends.* Staten Island, NY: Wisdom Pages, 2005. A how-to guide to help children learn how to cope with and disarm bullies. Kalman argues that many antibullying programs do not work because the programs try to teach bullies not to be bullies, instead of teaching bullied children not to be victims.

Cecile Maghari, *Bullying . . . Deal With It! A Self-Help Guide Detailing Techniques on How to Combat the Aftereffect of School Bullying and How to Do Home Education Learning.* Frederick, MD: PublishAmerica, 2007. The author explores the short- and long-term effects of bullying, as well as methods to use to deal with the damage it causes.

Katia Petersen, *Safe & Caring Schools: A Social/Emotional Resource Guide to Improve Academic Success and School Climate, Grades 6–8.* San Francisco, CA: Petersen Argo, 2005. Using the Social, Emotional, and Academic Learning (SEAL) formula, the author examines how positive character education, teaching kids to appreciate learning and school, can create a better and safer school environment for kids.

Dickon Pownall-Gray, *Susana's Struggle: A True Bullying Story.* Lulu.com, 2007. Based on a true story, this workbook offers approaches and suggestions for dealing with bullies, as well as showing teens how to become better leaders.

Walter B. Roberts Jr., *Bullying from Both Sides: Strategic Interventions for Working with Bullies and Victims.* Thousand Oaks, CA: Corwin Press, 2006. Discusses students who might be likely bullies or targets of bullying, as well as how to keep students safe, how to handle girls who bully, and how to counsel for short- and long-term assistance.

Rachel Simmons, *Odd Girl Speaks Out: Girls Write About Bullies, Cliques, Popularity, and Jealousy.* New York: Harvest Books, 2004. A compilation of essays in which girls write about their experiences being bullied, and the effects on them.

Barbara Trolley, Constance Hanel, and Linda L. Shields, *Demystifying and Deescalating Cyber Bullying in Schools: A Resource Guide for Counselors, Educators and Parents.* Bangor, ME: Booklocker.com, 2006. A resource guide to handling cyberbullying, including a variety of psychological, social, and educational interventions, and policies and procedures.

Joel Turtel, *Public Schools, Public Menace: How Public Schools Lie to Parents and Betray Our Children.* Staten Island, NY: Liberty Books, 2005. The author discusses the inadequate job that schools are doing in educating and protecting children, and explains how homeschooling can be successfully achieved.

Periodicals

Jacqueline Adams, "What Makes a Bully Tick? Scientists Search for Answers," *Science World*, October 23, 2006.

Advocate, "By the Numbers: School Bullying," November 22, 2005.

Parry Aftab, "Online Safety at School: Bullies and Other School Predators Have Entered Cyberspace, But You Can Help Thwart Them," *PC Magazine*, August 3, 2004.

Tara Anderson and Brian Sturm, "Cyberbullying: From Playground to Computer," *Young Adult Library Services*, Winter 2007.

Louise Arseneault, "Bullying Leaves Mark on Kids' Psyches," *Science News*, July 29, 2006.

Shaun Bailey, "Carrying a Knife Is No Longer the Exception—It's the Rule," *Telegraph*, January 6, 2006.

Jarrett T. Barrios and Robert A. Antonioni, "Bullying Is No Game," *Boston Globe*, September 20, 2005.

Rebecca Bria, "Anti-Bullying Policy Might Be Mandatory," *Knight Ridder Tribune Business News*, August 8, 2006.

Sabrina A. Brinson, "Boys Don't Tell on Sugar-and-Spice-But-Not-So-Nice Girl Bullies," *Reclaiming Children and Youth*, Fall 2005.

Helen Carter, "School Bully's Parents Get Life for Fire That Killed Family of Victim," *Guardian*, December 21, 2006.

D. Aileen Dodd, "Keeping the Peace: Help Kids Overcome Bullying Experiences," *Atlanta Journal-Constitution*, February 2, 2007.

Michael Dorn, "Beyond Bullying Programs," *School Planning and Management*, November 2005.

Odvard Egil Dyrli, "Cyberbullying: Online Bullying Affects Every School District," *District Administration*, September 2005.

Melanie Falcon, "Adopt-a-Bully Program," *Law & Order*, February 2004.

Lisa Feder-Feitel, "Bye-Bye Bullies!" *Scholastic Scope*, February 9, 2004.

Charlie Gillis, "You Have Hate Mail," *Maclean's*, January 9, 2006.

Jodie Gilmore, "HSLDA (Home School Legal Defense Association) Gets Family Out of Hot Water," *New American*, March 6, 2006.

Carmen Greco Jr., "Author Calls for Course to Curb School Bullying," *Chicago Tribune*, January 28, 2006.

Michael B. Greene, "Bullying in Schools: A Plea for Measure of Human Rights," *Journal of Social Issues*, 2006.

Eric Gwin, "Big, Bad 'Bully': Will This Video Game Make Your Kids Mean?" *Chicago Tribune*, November 1, 2006.

Mary Harvey, "Bullies Beware: How One School Stood Up to Bullies," *Junior Scholastic*, February 6, 2006.

Marianne D. Hurst, "When It Comes to Bullying, There Are No Boundaries," *Education Week*, February 9, 2005.

Kay S. Hymowitz, "Silly Laws Are No Way to Fight Bullying," *Los Angeles Times*, April 18, 2004.

Internet Week, "Cyberbullying Eyed as Latest E-Threat by Washington," May 25, 2005.

Raviya H. Ismail, "Anti-Bullying Bill Stalls in Senate Committee: Republican Leaders Say Law Not Needed, Won't Solve Problem," *Knight Ridder Tribune Business News*, March 23, 2006.

Dean P. Johnson, "Schools Are Banning Tag. What's Next: Musical Chairs?" *Christian Science Monitor*, November 3, 2006.

Jaana Juvonen, "Myths and Facts About Bullying in Schools: Effective Interventions Depend Upon Debunking Long-Held Misconceptions," *Behavioral Health Management*, March–April 2005.

Raymond J. Keating, "Parents Need to Protect Kids on Net," *Newsday*, January 22, 2007.

Andreas Kelly and Kevin Smith, "New Anti-Bullying Law Not the Final Answer," *Arizona Daily Star*, December 15, 2005.

Jessie Klein, "If Cho Had Not Been Bullied . . ." *Newsday*, April 27, 2007.

Josh Korr, "It's Called the First Amendment, Mr. Thompson," *St. Petersburg Times*, October 12, 2006.

Jennifer Kroll, "Bullies Can Be Beat," *Current Health 1*, January 2006.

Antony Lane, "Learn to Be a Bully," *New Statesman*, October 30, 2006.

James Lehmann, "Allowing Bullying," *Chicago Tribune*, December 11, 2004.

Ilene Lelchuk, "School Bullies' New Tuff: Internet/Taunted Novato Girl's Plight Illustrates Painful Phenomenon," *San Francisco Chronicle*, March 17, 2007.

Shawn D. Lewis, "Michigan Lawmakers Take on School Bullies: There's No State Standard on Issue," *Detroit News*, September 19, 2006.

Christopher Lowe, "Selfish Showoffs," *Newsday*, January 28, 2007.

Adam Luck, "50 Ways to Tackle Bullies," *Times Educational Supplement*, September 23, 2005.

Farhad Manjoo, "The Video Game Bullies," *Salon.com*, November 11, 2006.

Patrick McCormick, "Pick on Someone Your Own Size!" *U.S. Catholic*, September 2005.

Barbara Meltz, "Picking a Fight: 'Bully' Rekindles the Debate over Video Games and School Violence," *Boston Globe*, October 21, 2006.

Joe Menard and Mike Martindale, "Bullying Can Push Students over the Edge," *Detroit News*, March 25, 2005.

Lori Nudo, "Fighting the Real Bullies," *Prevention*, November 2004.

Megan O'Rourke, "Basic Brutality," *Newsday*, January 28, 2007.

J.W. Patchin and S. Hinduja, "Bullies Move Beyond the Schoolyard: A Preliminary Look at Cyberbullying," *Youth Violence and Juvenile Justice* 4, no. 2 (2006).

Robert Pigott, "Ugly Example," *Newsday*, January 28, 2007.

Sean Price, "The Problem with Bullies: For Teens All over the U.S., Bullying Has Become a Serious Health Crisis," *Junior Scholastic*, February 9, 2004.

Robert D. Ramsey, "Direct Intervention on an Increasing Problem," *Supervision*, December 2005.

Michael Reist, "Unspoken Truth About Bullying," *Catholic New Times*, April 23, 2006.

Denise Rinaldo, "Cool to Be Cruel? Bullying Is a Popular Activity in Schools, But One Woman, Who Was Tormented in Her Youth, Is Working to Change That," *Scholastic Choices*, April–May 2004.

Kelly Salloum, "Carried Away," *Newsday*, January 28, 2007.

Joy Scanlon, "Boy Trouble," *Newsday*, January 28, 2007.

Thomas B. Scheffey, "Bullying Victim Has No Redress," *Connecticut Law Tribune*, September 11, 2006.

Joshua A. Schiering, "Bullying Prevention Taken to New Heights at Camp Sewataro," *Camping Magazine*, March–April 2005.

Scholastic Parent and Child, "Dealing with Bullying," December 2006.

Derek Simon, "Low Entertainment," *Newsday*, January 28, 2007.

Dana Slagle, "How to Prevent Bullies from Terrorizing Your Child," *Jet*, January 29, 2007.

Shepherd Smith, "Teenage Bullying and Violence: Is There a Cure?" *Youth Connection*, January–February 2005.

Heidi Spletc, "Academic Problems Beget Bullying," *Clinical Psychiatry News*, December 2005.

Matthew Taylor, "Twelve Years Later, a Pupil Tormented by Primary School Bullies Gets 20,000 Pounds: Local Authorities Fear Case May Set Precedent; Years of Taunts and Attacks Led to Suicide Attempt," *Guardian*, February 21, 2006.

U.S. Federal News Service, "Can School Bullying Have Deadly Consequences?" October 27, 2006.

Peggy Walsh-Sarnecki, "Outraged Teens Fight Against Violent Game," *Knight Ridder Tribune Business News*, September 29, 2005.

Lucy Ward, "Violent Films Fuel School Bullying, Says Puttnam," *Guardian*, April 19, 2005.

Sonia Whalen-Miller, "Why Wasn't I Invited?" *Maclean's*, August 7, 2006.

Michael Winerip, "Feeling a Child's Pain, and Reliving Your Own," *New York Times*, January 21, 2007.

Web Sites

Centers for Disease Control and Prevention, National Center for Injury Prevention and Control, National Academic Centers of Excellence on Youth Violence Prevention (www.cdc.gov/ncipc/res -opps/ACE/ace.htm). The Centers for Disease Control and Prevention funded ten universities to research and create anti-youth-violence programs, including bullying prevention. The Web site includes data and statistics, as well as research.

National Youth Violence Prevention Resource Center (www.safeyouth .org). Sponsored by the Centers for Disease Control and Prevention and other federal agencies, the National Youth Violence Prevention Resource Center's Web site offers a central directory of resources for a variety of issues affecting children, including bullying. These resources include publications, fact sheets, research, statistics, and prevention and intervention programs.

Stop Bullying Now! (www.stopbullyingnow.hrsa.gov). A project of the U.S. Department of Health and Human Services' Human Resources and Services Administration, the Stop Bullying Now! Web site is devoted to helping kids learn what they can do to help stop bullying. There are Webisodes that deal with bullying; advice on dealing with bullying, whether you are the bully, the bullied, or a bystander; a chance to send in questions and participate in online polls; and information for parents.

Index

Picture Credits

Cover: © Corbis
Jaimie Trueblood/CBS Photo Archive via Getty Images, 12
AP Images, 14, 19, 44, 48, 54, 63, 70, 79, 81, 95, 100
Joe Raedle/Newsmakers, 27
Acey Harper/Time Life Pictures/Getty Images, 31, 88
© Shout/Alamy, 37
Tim Boyle/Getty Images, 40
Melanie Stetson Freeman/The Christian Science Monitor via Getty Images, 60
Carolyn Schaefer/Liaison, 76